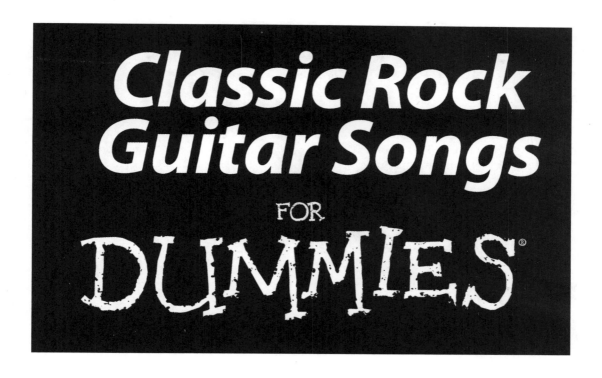

# Classic Rock Guitar Songs

## FOR DUMMIES

**Performance Notes by Adam Perlmutter**

ISBN 978-1-4234-9576-5

HAL•LEONARD®
CORPORATION

7777 W. BLUEMOUND RD. P.O. BOX 13819 MILWAUKEE, WI 53213

Visit Hal Leonard Online at
**www.halleonard.com**

# Table of Contents

# Introduction

. . . . . . . . . . . . . . . . . . . . . . . . . . . . . . . . . . . . . . . . . . . . . . . . . . . . .

*W*elcome to *Classic Rock Guitar Songs For Dummies*. In this book, you'll find everything you need to play some great classic rock songs, from John Cougar Mellencamp's "Authority Song" to ZZ Top's "La Grange" to Cream's "White Room." Included throughout are some handy performance notes that will show you exactly how to play the songs and how they work. In reading the transcriptions and the notes, you'll learn how to play some essential guitar techniques: hammer-ons, pull-offs, slides, bends, and more. Not only that, each song's performance note includes some background information, for a bit of rock 'n' roll trivia.

Although this book acts as an instructional tool to learn these classic rock and pop tunes, it's not a guitar method, and may be too advanced for absolute beginners. If you're picking up a guitar for the first time, try *Guitar For Dummies,* 2nd Edition by Mark Phillips and Jon Chappell (Wiley), and then come back to *Classic Rock Guitar Songs For Dummies*.

## About This Book

For every song, you get a brief intro with a little background on the artist (in case you're not already a rock trivia god), followed by the essential info you need to learn the song:

- ✔ A run-down of the parts you need to know, not including those parts that are clones of other sections of the song.
- ✔ A breakdown of some of the special techniques you need to play the song — the trade secrets you won't see on the sheet music.
- ✔ When necessary, some info you need to navigate the sheet music (such as pickup measures). Be sure to familiarize yourself with codas, repeats, and other navigational details explained in the Guitar Notation Legend.

You may already know a lot of this stuff, so if you know it, skip it — unless you find the writing especially witty and eloquent (yeah, right). The best strategy is always to go through the song and find all the main chords and their positions (the chord chart at the back will help), then try working in all the licks and tricks.

## How to Use This Book

The music in this book is in standard notation and *tablature* (also known as *tab*) — which is just a diagram of the guitar strings with numbers that tell you what frets to play. Assuming you know a little something about reading tab or music, the Guitar Notation Legend in the back helps translate all those strange words, alien symbols, and hieroglyphs that are the written language of guitarheads. I also assume you know some things about the guitar itself — like how to hold it, where the neck and frets are, how to tune it, basic chord strumming, and how to look cool while doing it.

There's also a chart of common chords and scale positions in the back. This is handy, because where a line of tab gives you fret numbers, these diagrams show you the visual shape of the chords and scales and which fingers work best for them.

New techniques and concepts are introduced as they appear, and referred back to when necessary. So you can skip around the book and pick out your favorite songs first, without missing out on essential information.

## Conventions used in this book

Here are some common rock guitar terms you'll see discussed throughout the book:

- ✔ **Barre chords** (chords in which one finger holds down a few strings at once)
- ✔ **Open strings** (strings played in **open position**, without a finger holding them down)
- ✔ **Riffs** (repeating bits of music that are noteworthy enough to mention) and **licks**, (common lead guitar tricks)
- ✔ **Strumming** (using a guitar pick to "fling" across the strings, often in a pattern of **downstrokes** — strumming down toward the earth — and **upstrokes** toward the sky)
- ✔ **Power chords** (those chunky two-note chords, labeled with a "5," that make rock what it is)
- ✔ **Pentatonic** (five-note) **scales** (the basis for most of the hot licks and screaming solos you're about to learn)
- ✔ **Other terms** that are explained in the Guitar Notation Legend. In the performance notes, when you see an unfamiliar word in italics, that's your cue to flip to the back of the book.

## Your other left

No two guitarists are the same, and some of the greatest ones happen to play left-handed — so forgive your author/teacher for sometimes referring to the picking hand as "right" and the fretting hand as "left." Sometimes there's no better way to say it.

## Down is up

When I talk about low and high strings, I'm talking pitch-wise, in terms of what you hear, not what you see. Your low E string, for example, is the string on "top," the fattest one with the lowest sound (sometimes tuned down to D or lower). The high E string is the skinny one on the "bottom," and so on. I try to be as clear as possible on whether I'm talking about sound or sight. Speaking of which, the names of the open strings in standard tuning, low to high, are E–A–D–G–B–E.

# Icons Used in This Book

In the margins of this book are lots of little icons that will help make your life easier:

Optional parts, like insanely fast solos, that may be too challenging for many guitarists, but are discussed anyway for the learned and/or ambitious "champion" players among you. There's no way to walk you through every lick, but you'll get some tips that might make them less painful. In these discussions I may have to throw lots of strange terms at you, all of which can be found in the Guitar Notation Legend.

Details (such as tunings and special techniques) that you need to know, and will probably need again in the future.

Notes about specific musical concepts that are relevant but confusing to the layperson. Sometimes it's just something that's musically very cool!

Shortcuts and suggested ways to get through some of the hard parts without tangling your fingers.

A reason to stop and review advice that can prevent damage to your fingers, ears, guitar, or ego.

# *Aqualung*

Music by Ian Anderson
Words by Jennie Anderson

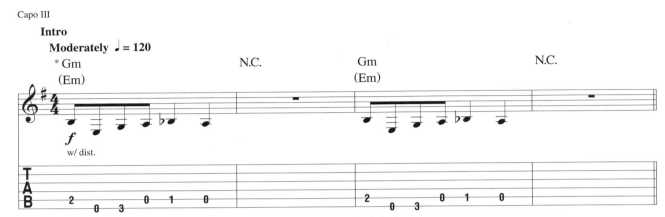

*Symbols in parentheses represent chord names respective to capoed guitar. Symbols above reflect actual sounding chords. Capoed fret is "0" in tab.

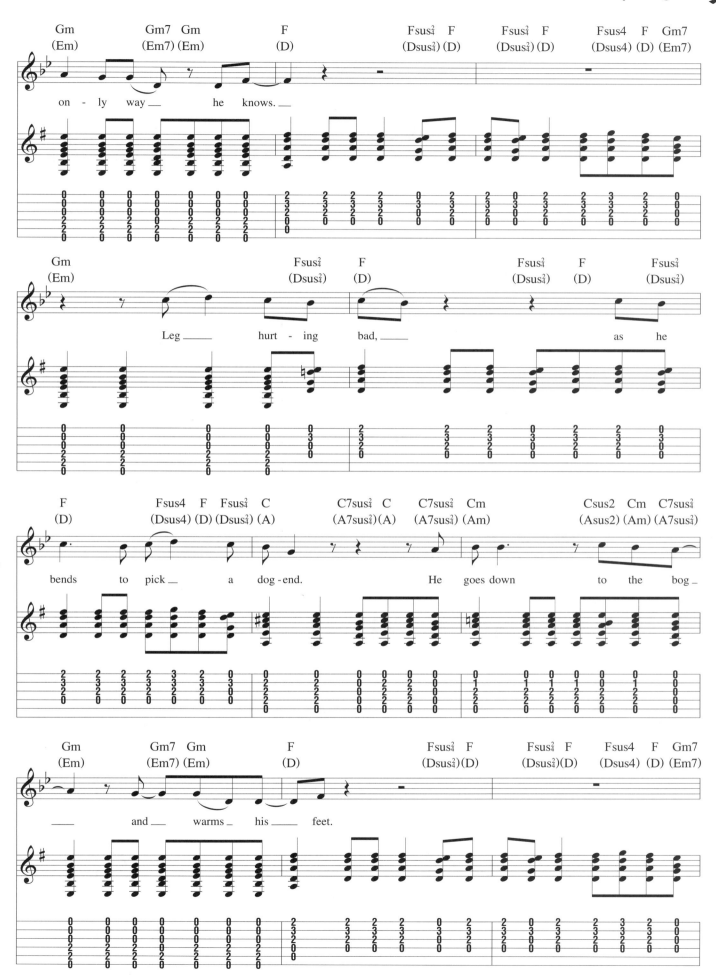

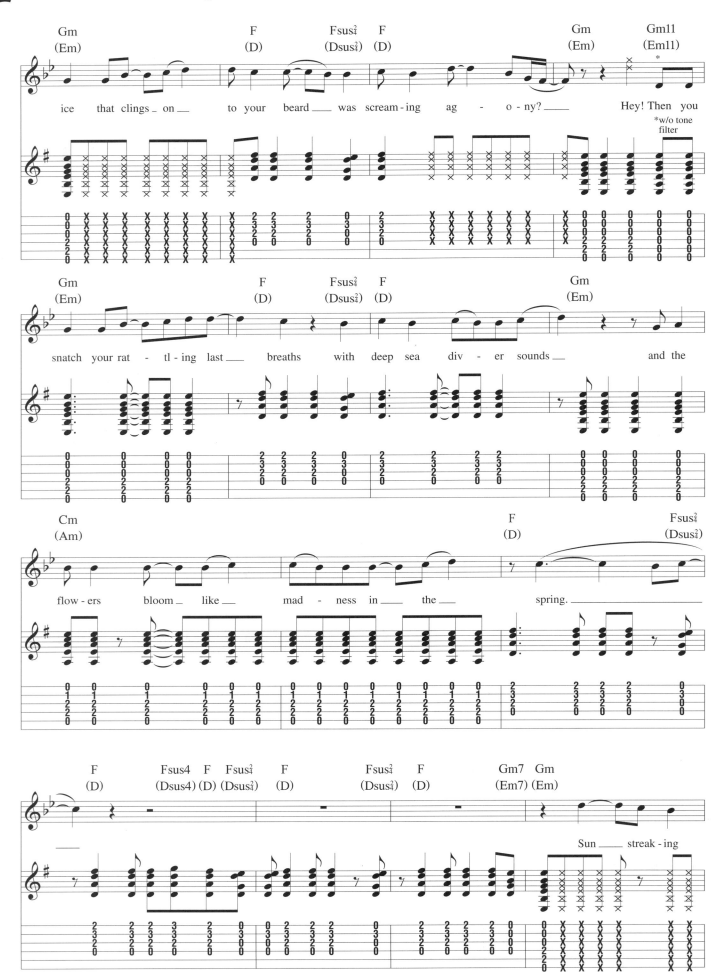

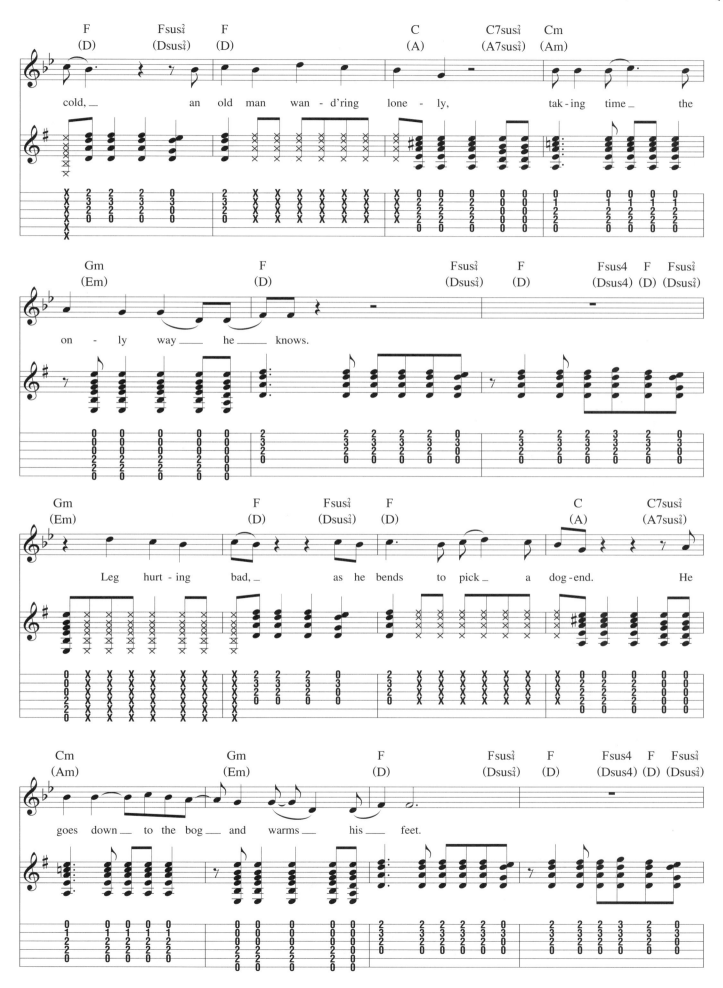

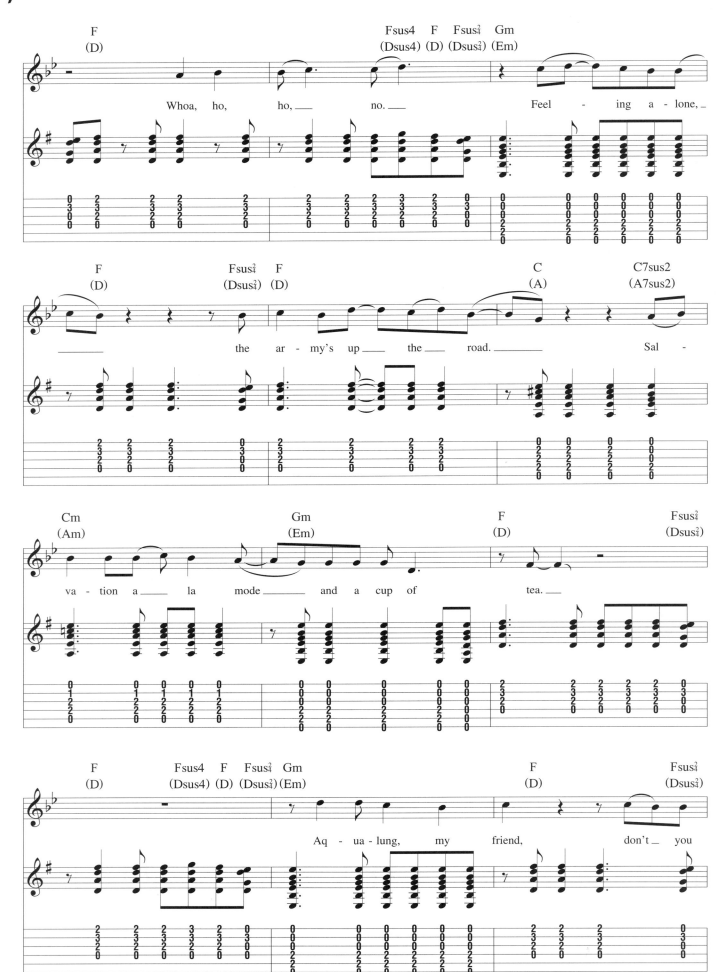

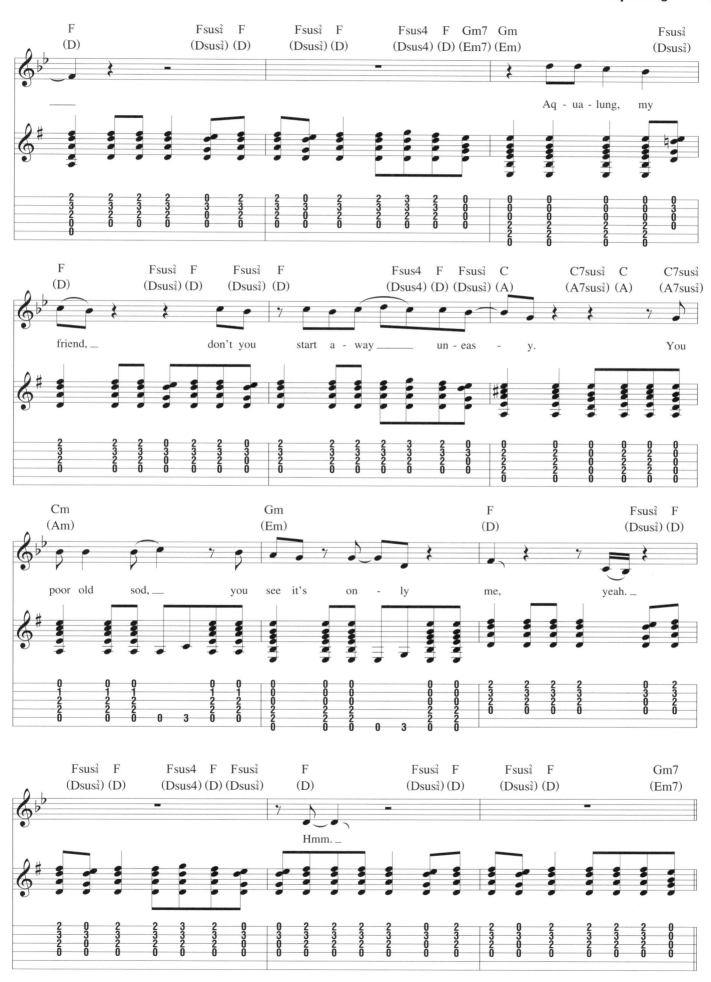

*D.S. al Coda*

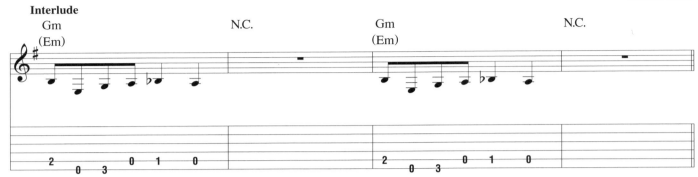

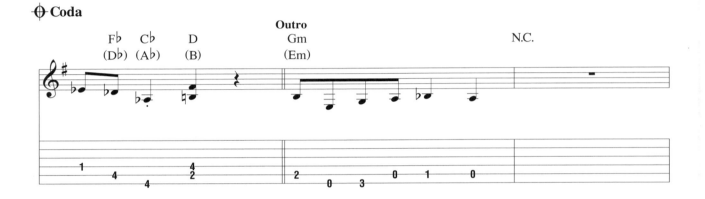

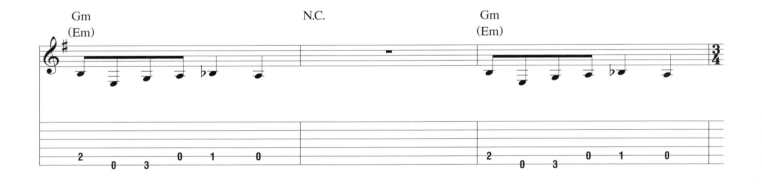

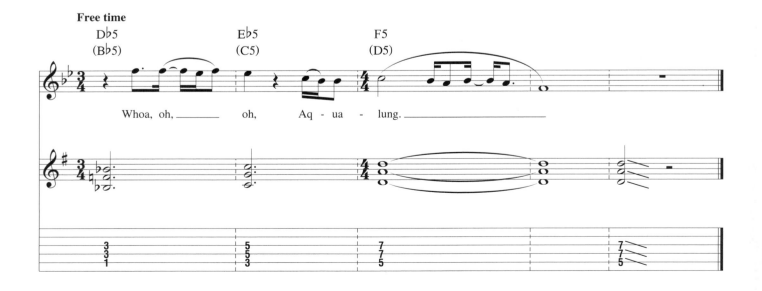

# Authority Song

### Words and Music by
### John Mellencamp

Double drop D tuning:
(low to high) D-A-D-G-B-D

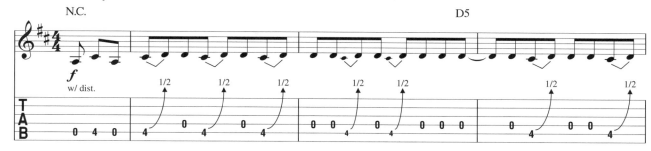

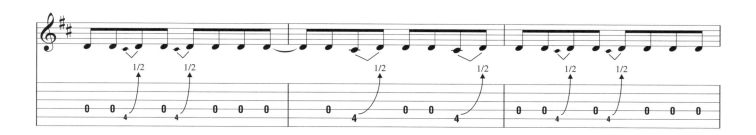

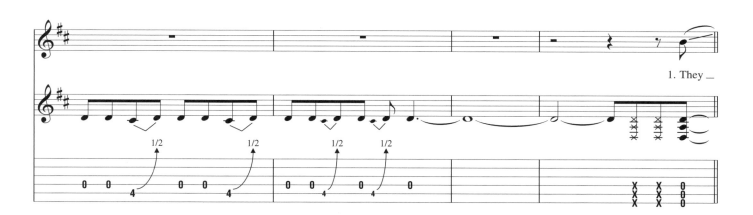

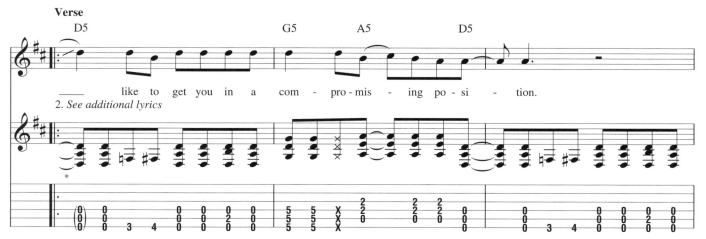

\* 2nd time, tie bottom note only.

Well, I _____ fight au - thor - i - ty, au - thor - i - ty al - ways wins. _____

Oh, yeah. _____

Interlude

Guitar Solo

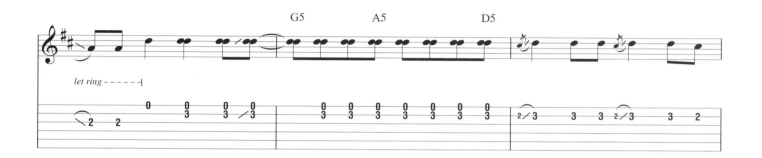

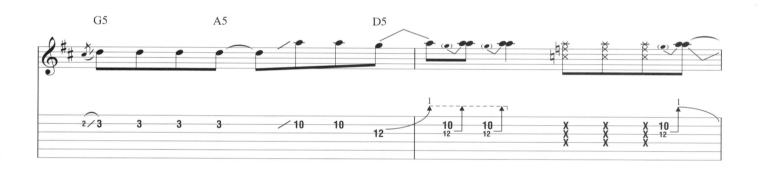

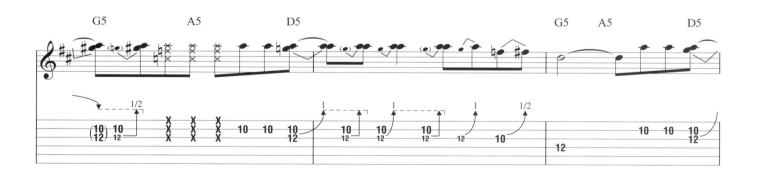

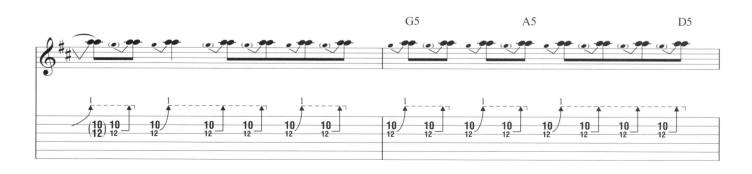

I say, oh, ____

**Interlude**

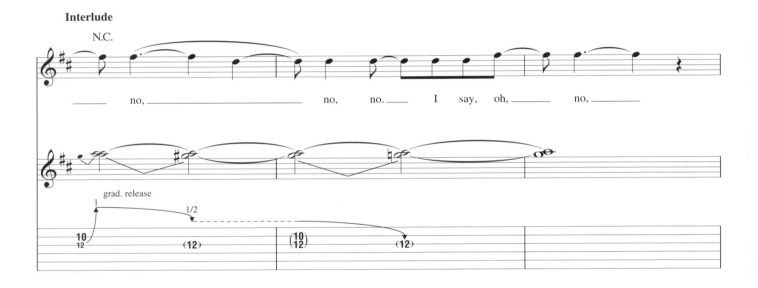

____ no, ____ no, no. ____ I say, oh, ____ no, ____

no, no. ____ I say, oh, ____ no, ____ no, ____ no, no. ____ I

**Outro-Chorus**

fight au - thor - i - ty, au - thor - i - ty al - ways wins. ____ I ____

____ fight au - thor - i - ty, au - thor - i - ty al - ways wins. ____ Kick it in.

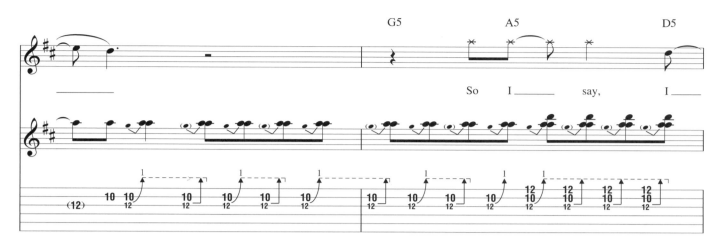

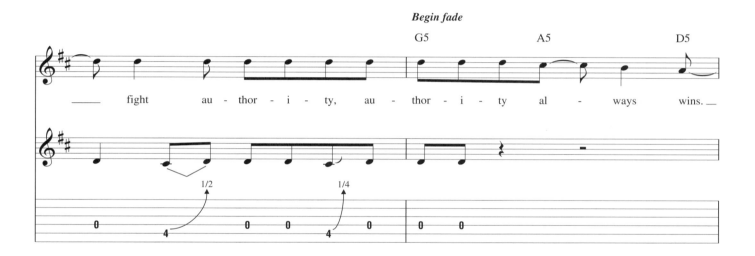

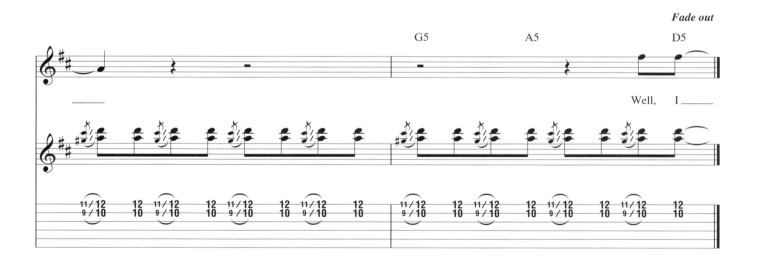

*Additional Lyrics*

2. I call up my preacher, I say, "Give me strength for round five."
   He said, "You don't need no strength, you need to grow up, son."
   I said, "Growing up leads to growing old and then to dying.
   Ooh, and dying to me don't sound like all that much fun."
   And so I say,...

# Bad Case of Loving You

Words and Music by John Moon Martin

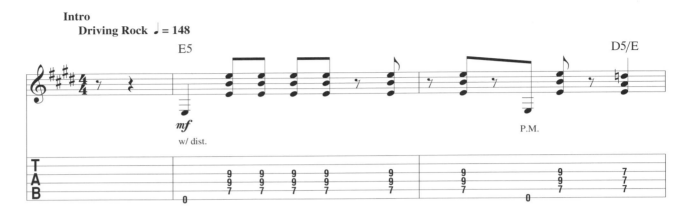

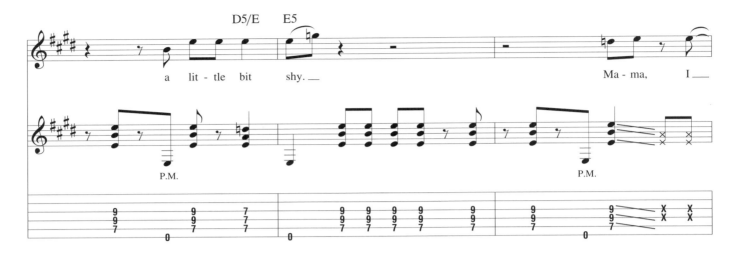

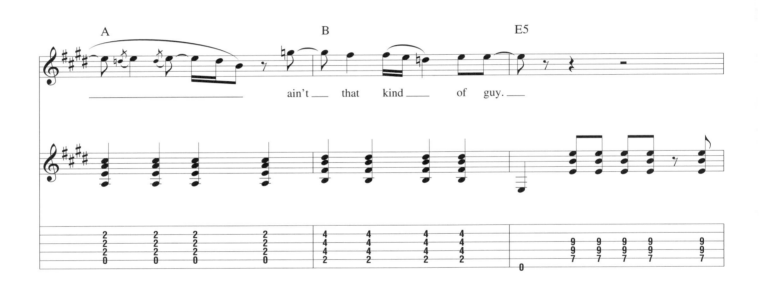

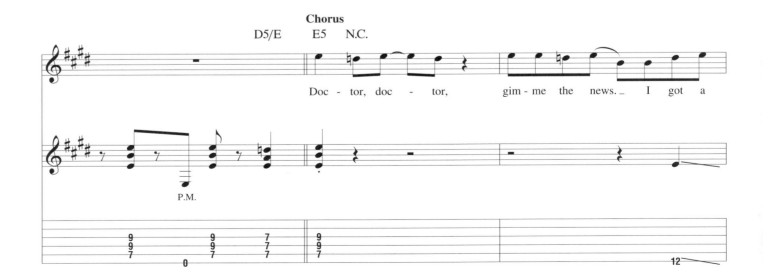

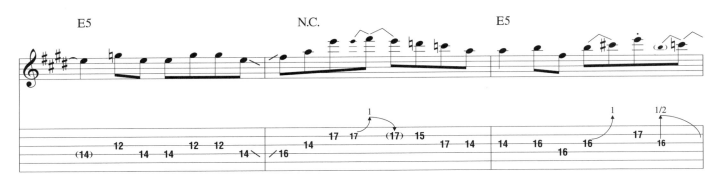

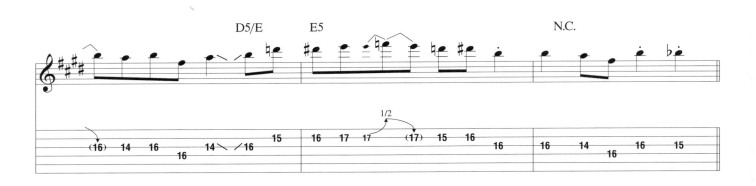

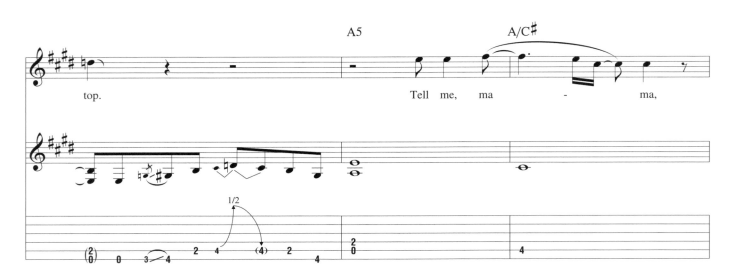

B

are you gon - na stop? _____

**Interlude**

E5                                                                D5/E    E5

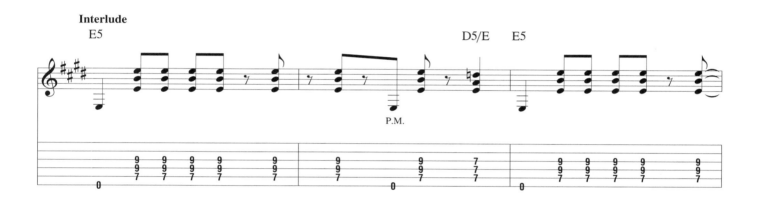

P.M.

*D.S. al Coda*

✛ **Coda**

E5

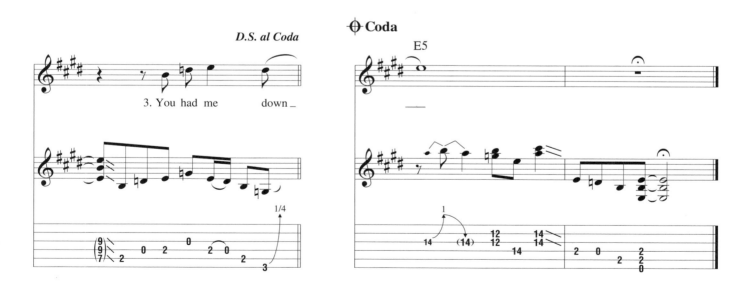

3. You had me        down _        _____

**Additional Lyrics**

3. You had me down, uh, twenty-one to zip,
   Smile of Judas on your lip.
   Shake my fist, knock on wood.
   I've got it bad and I got it good.

# Ballroom Blitz

Words and Music by Mike Chapman and Nicky Chinn

2nd time, substitute Fill 1

man    at the back,   as  a   mat - ter  of  fact. ___   His   eyes ___   are   as   red   as   the ___

Gtr. tacet

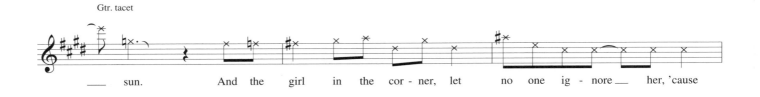

___ sun.      And   the   girl    in  the  cor - ner,   let      no   one   ig - nore ___  her,  'cause

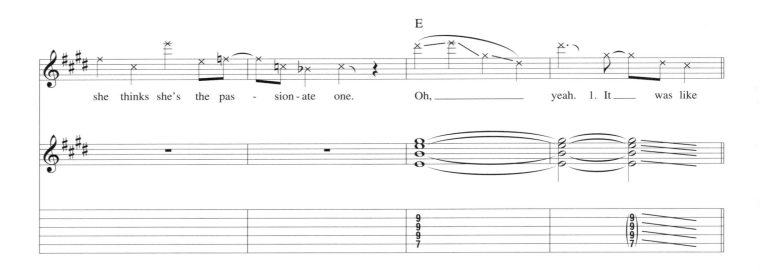

she  thinks  she's  the  pas  -  sion - ate   one.      Oh, _____   yeah.  1. It ___   was   like

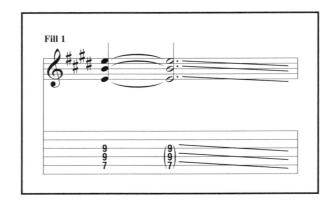

**Fill 1**

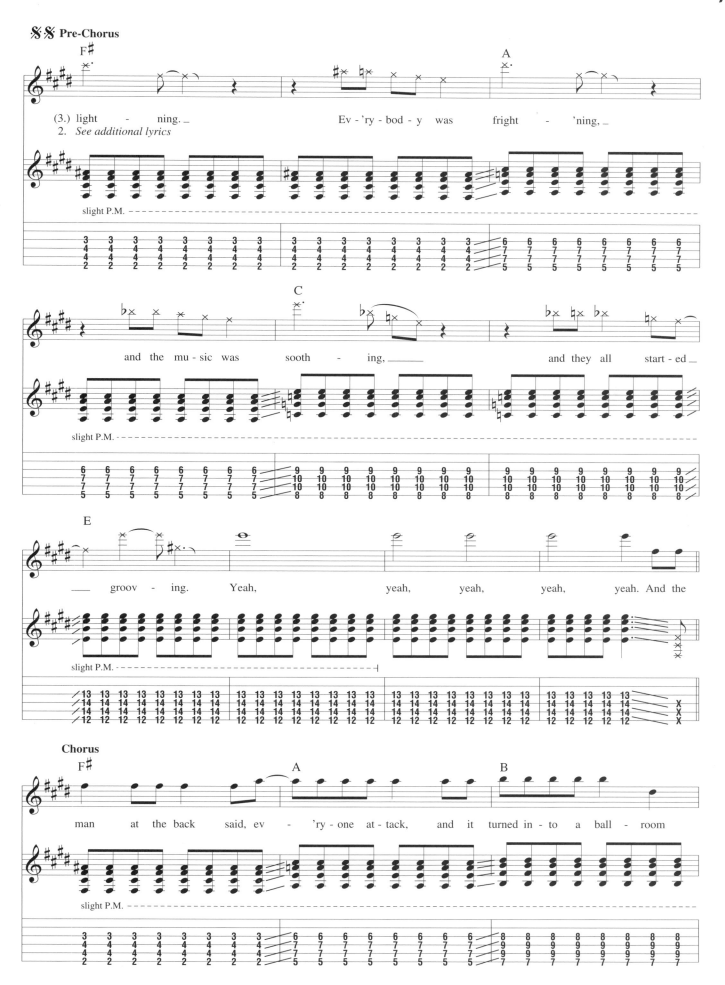

**Coda 1**

**Interlude**

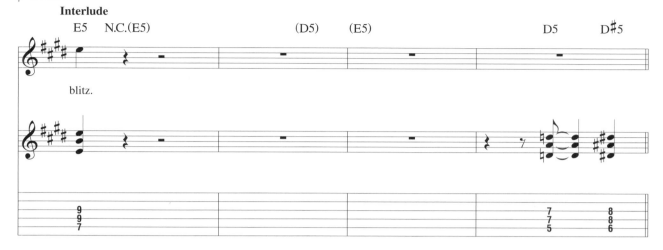

blitz.

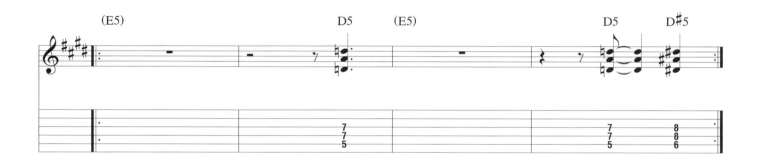

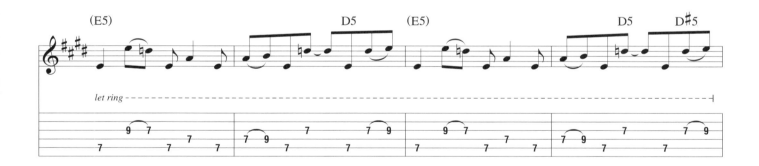

*let ring*

*D.S.S. al Coda 2*

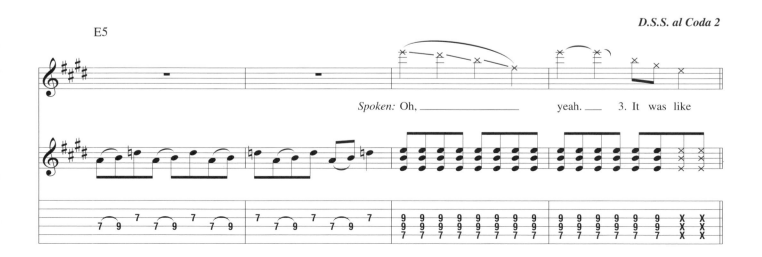

*Spoken:* Oh, _____ yeah. \_\_\_ 3. It was like

**Coda 2**

*Additional Lyrics*

2. Oh, I'm reachin' out for something; touching nothing's all I ever do.
   Oh, I softly call you over. When you appear, there's nothing left of you. Uh, huh.
   Now the man at the back is ready to crack as he raises his hands to the sky.
   And the girl in the corner is ev'ryone's mourner; she could kill you with a wink of her eye.
   Oh, yeah.

*Pre-Chorus* 2. It was electric, so frantic'ly hectic,
   And the band started leaping 'cause they all stopped breathing.
   Yeah, yeah, yeah, yeah, yeah.

# Bang a Gong (Get It On)

Words and Music by Marc Bolan

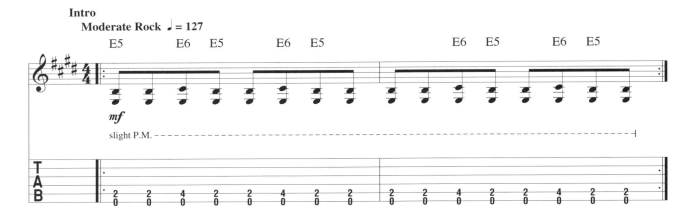

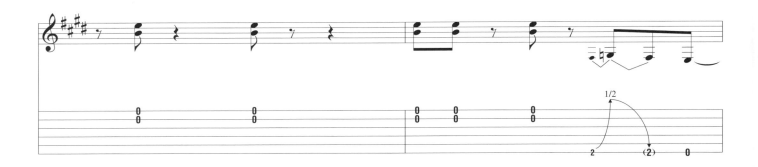

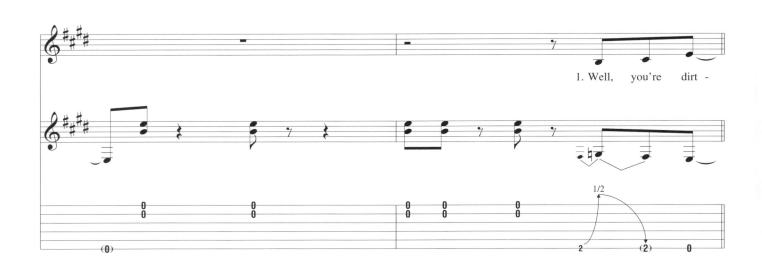

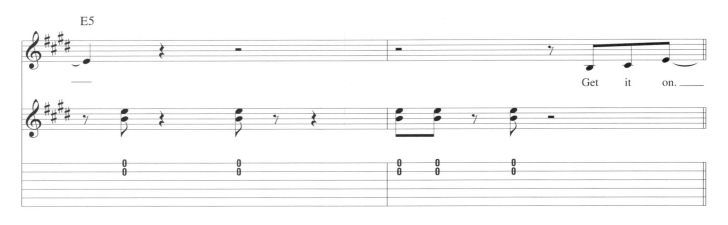

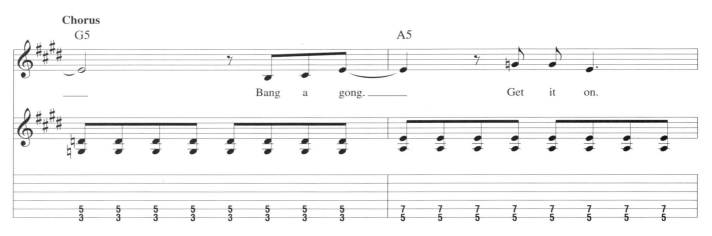

Chorus

Bang a gong._____ Get it on.

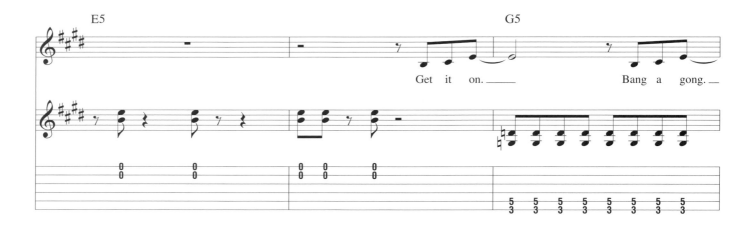

Get it on._____ Bang a gong._____

*To Coda* ⊕

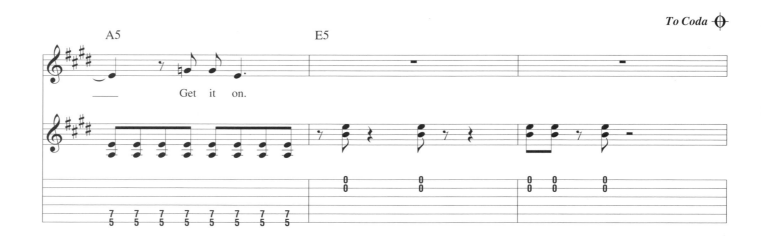

Get it on.

**Interlude**

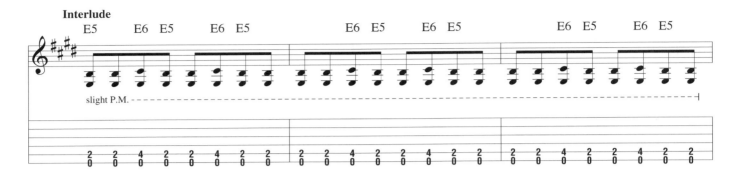

**Sax Break**

**Chorus**

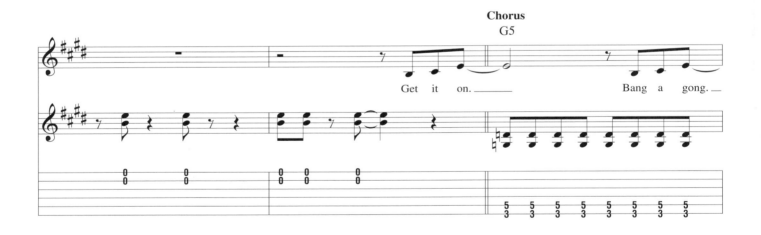

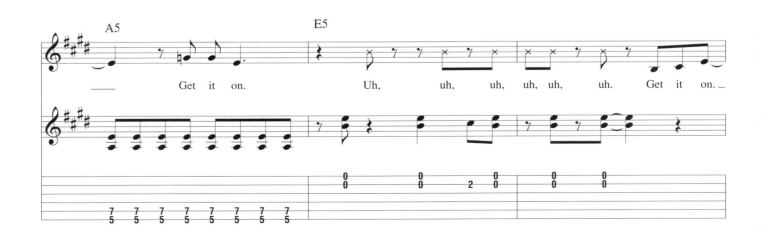

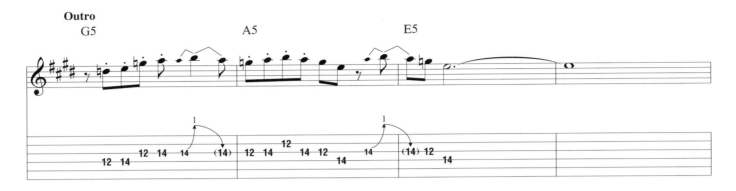

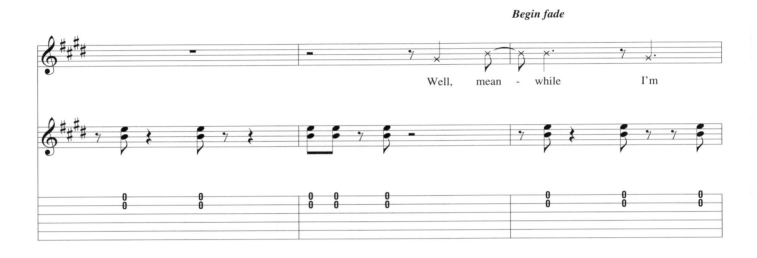

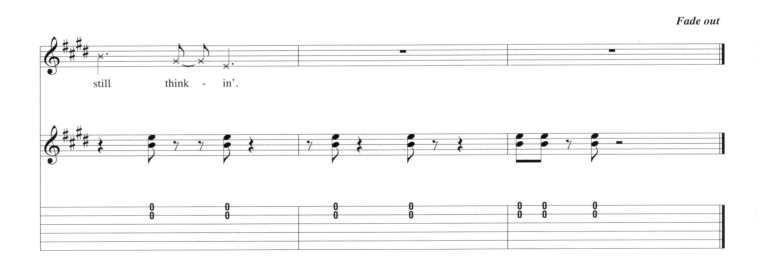

*Additional Lyrics*

3. Well, you're windy and wild, you've got the blues in your shoes and your stockings.
You're windy and wild, oh, yeah.
Well, you're built like a car, you've got a hubcap diamond star halo.
You're dirty, sweet and you're my girl.

# Deuce

Words and Music by Gene Simmons

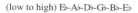

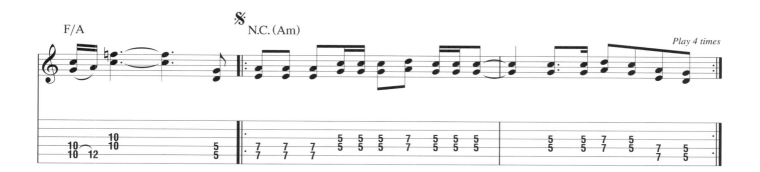

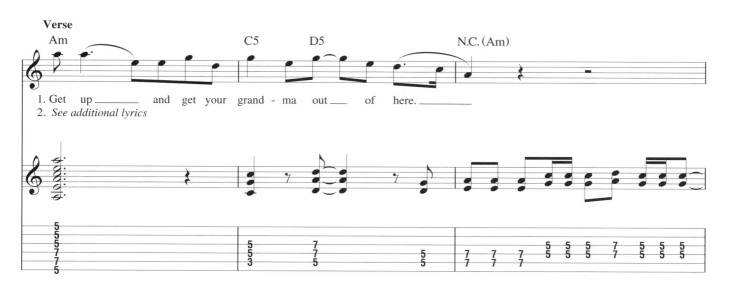

1. Get up _____ and get your grand - ma out ___ of here. ___
2. *See additional lyrics*

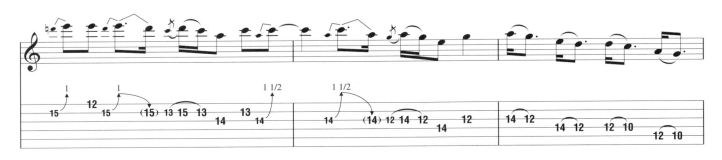

**Chorus**

N.C.

And,   ba - by,   if  you're feel - in' good,                    yes,

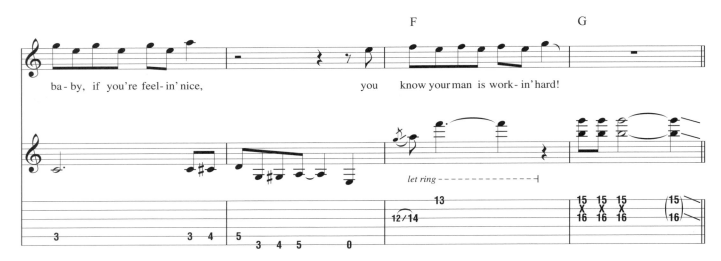

ba - by,  if  you're feel - in' nice,                    you    know your man is work - in' hard!

F                    G

let ring - - - - - - - - - - - -

**Interlude**

A5                              F/A          G/B                A5

let ring - - - - - - - - - - - - -                    let ring - - - - - - - - - - - - - -

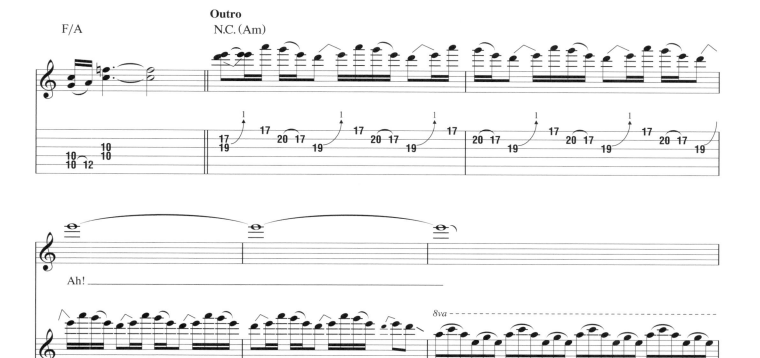

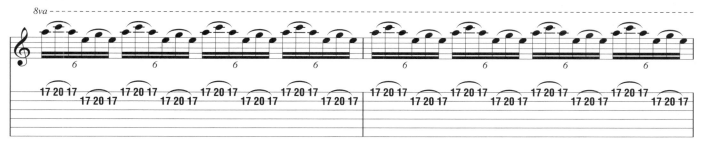

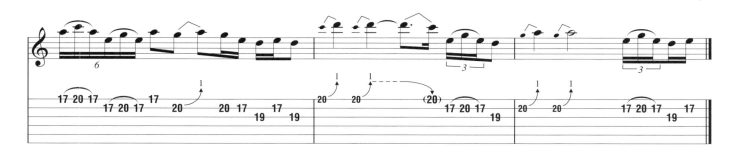

*Additional Lyrics*

2. Honey, don't push your man behind his years.
   And, baby, stop cryin' all your tears.
   Baby, do the things he says to do.
   Do it!

# Changes

Written by George "Buddy" Miles

Tune down 1/2 step:
(low to high) Eb-Ab-Db-Gb-Bb-Eb

**Intro**
**Moderate Rock** ♩ = 116

*w/ dist.

*Vol. knob rolled back.

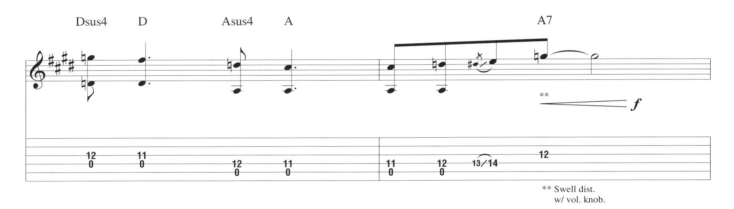

** Swell dist.
w/ vol. knob.

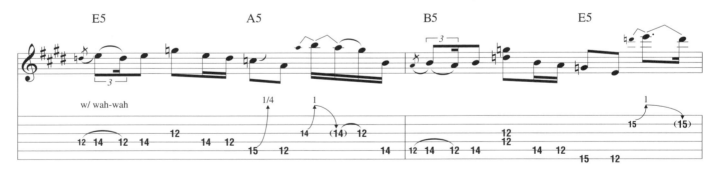

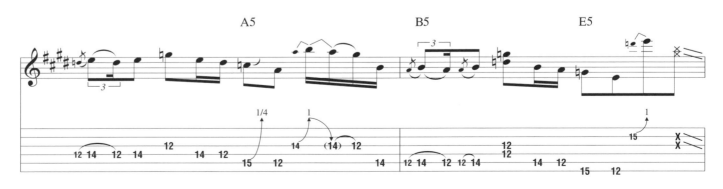

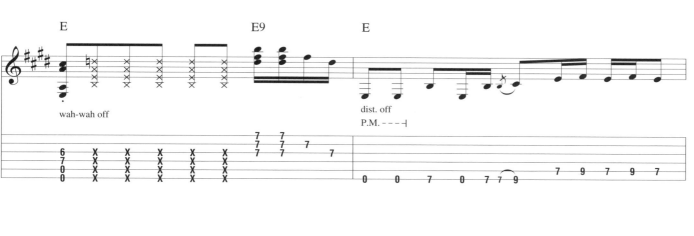

(Buddy Miles:) 1. Well, my

**Verse**

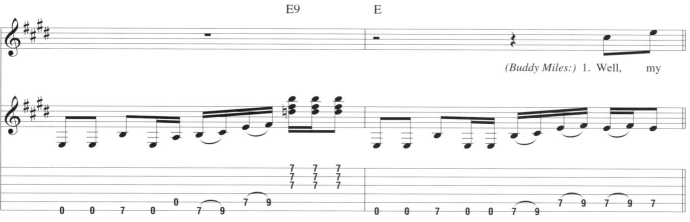

mind __ is go - in' through them chang - es, ____

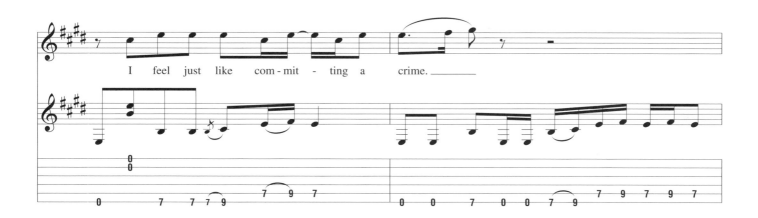

I feel just like com - mit - ting a crime. ____

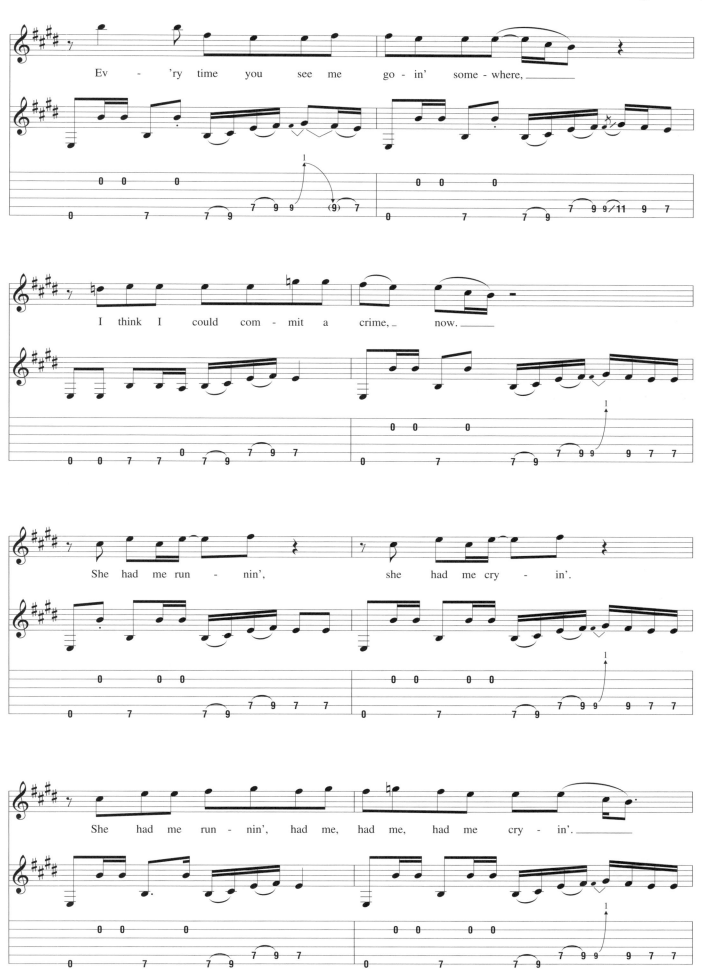

**Guitar Solo**

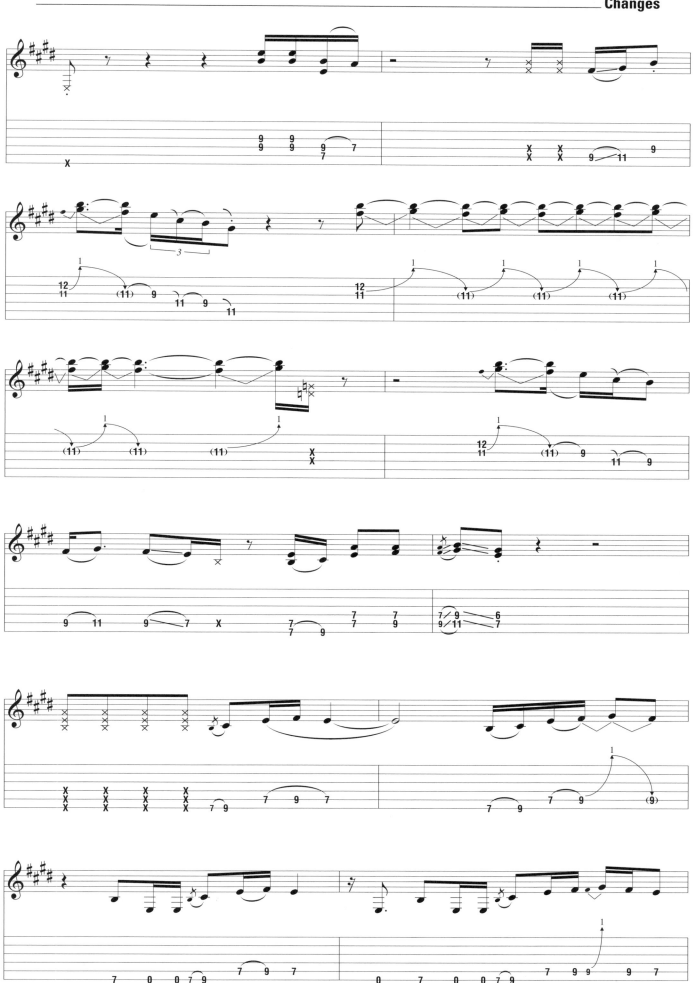

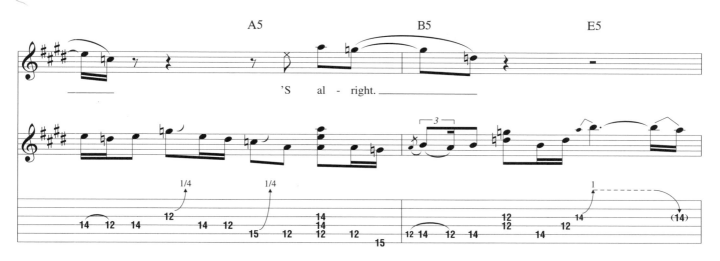

'S    al - right.

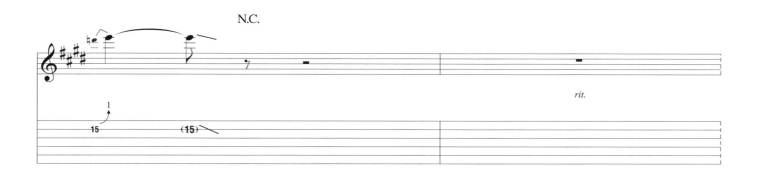

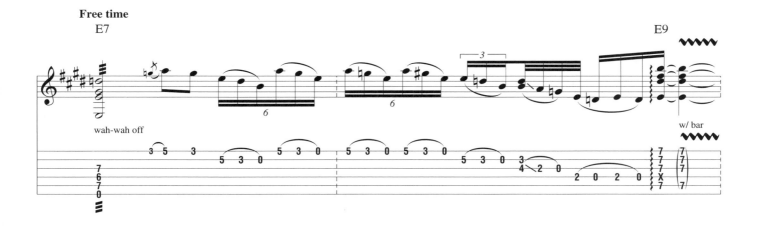

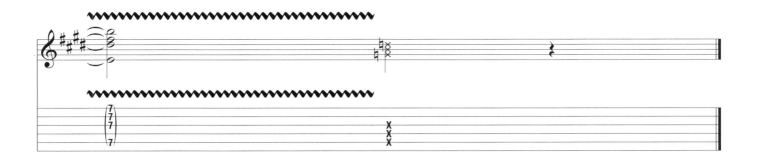

# Don't Ask Me No Questions

Words and Music by Ronnie Van Zant and Gary Rossington

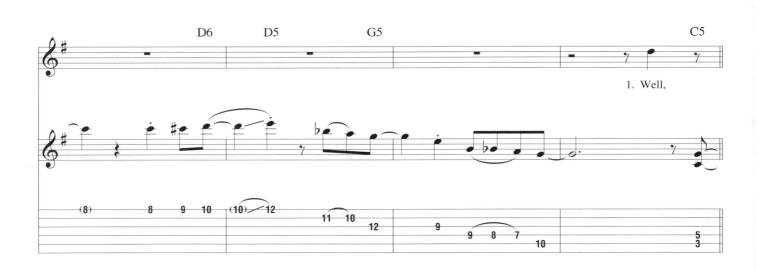

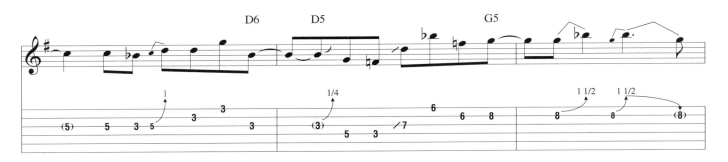

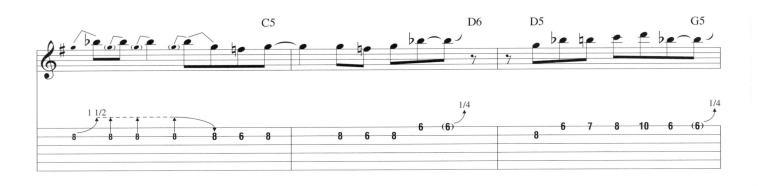

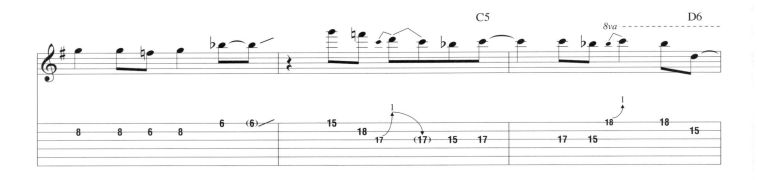

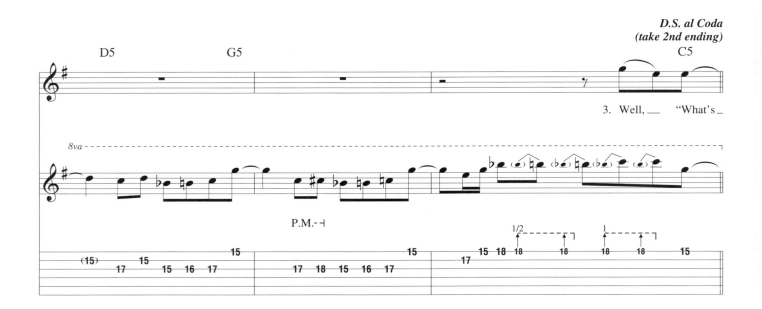

*Additional Lyrics*

2. Well, it's true I love the money
   And I love my brand new car.
   I like drinkin' the best of whiskey
   And playin' in a honky-tonk bar.
   But when I come off the road,
   Well, I just gotta have my time.
   'Cause I got to find a break in this action,
   Else I'm gonna lose my mind.

3. Well, "What's your fav'rite color and do you dig the brother,"
   Is drivin' me up the wall.
   And ev'ry time I think I can sleep
   Some fool has got to call.
   Well, don't you think that when I come home
   I just want a little peace of mind?
   If you want to talk about the business,
   Buddy, you just wastin' time.

# Funk #49

Words and Music by Joe Walsh, Dale Peters and James Fox

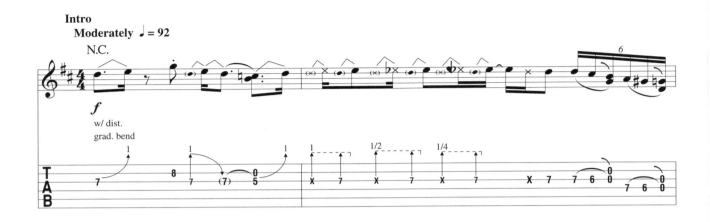

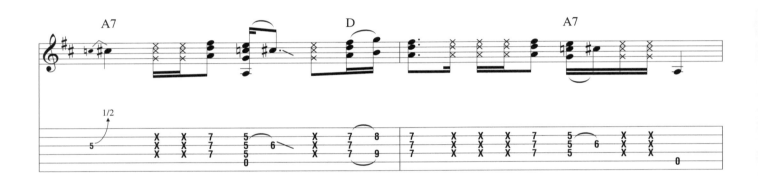

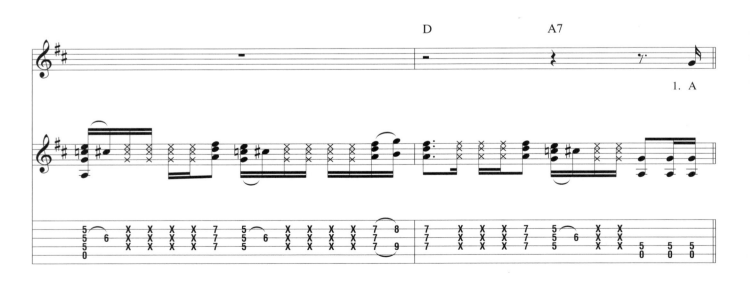

%  **Verse**

sleep all    day, __    out all    night, __    I   know   where   you're   go  -  in'.
2., 3. *See additional lyrics*

I    don't    think __    that's   act - in'    right, __    you   don't   think    it's   show  -  in'.

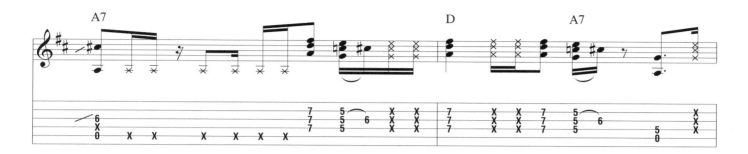

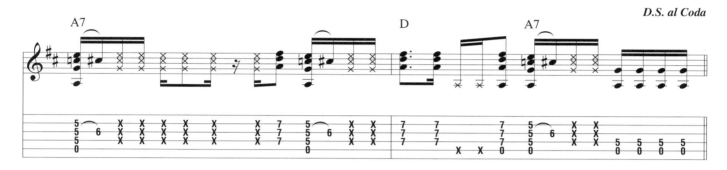

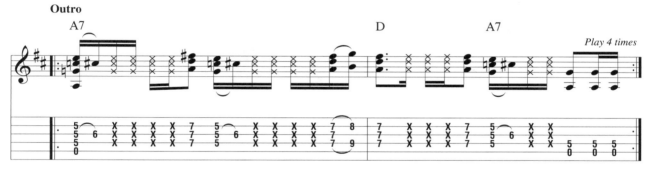

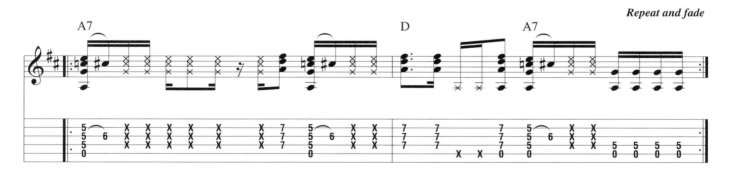

*Additional Lyrics*

2. A, jumpin' up, fallin' down,
Don't misunderstand me.
You don't think that I know your plan;
What you try'n' to hand me?

3. Out all night, sleep all day,
I know what you're doin'.
If you're gonna act this way,
I think there's trouble brewin'.

# Her Strut

Words and Music by Bob Seger

Tune down 1/2 step:
(low to high) E♭-A♭-D♭-G♭-B♭-E♭

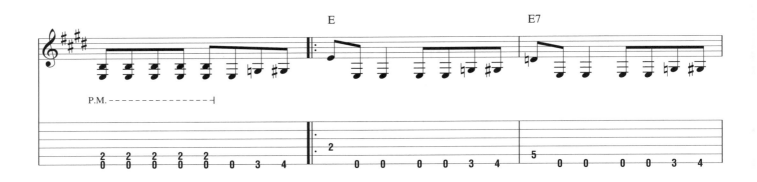

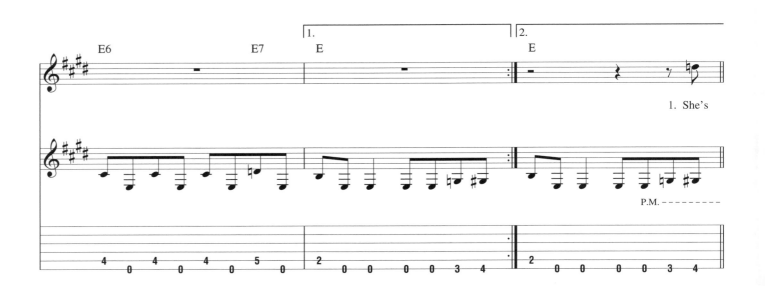

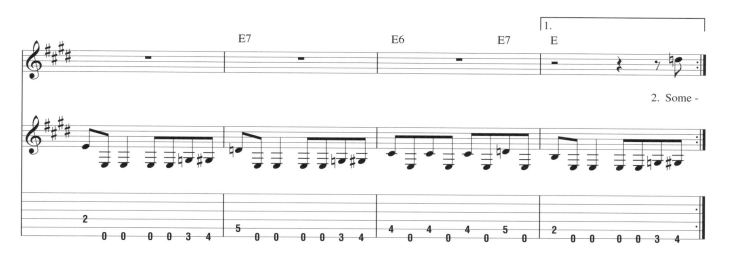

2. Some -

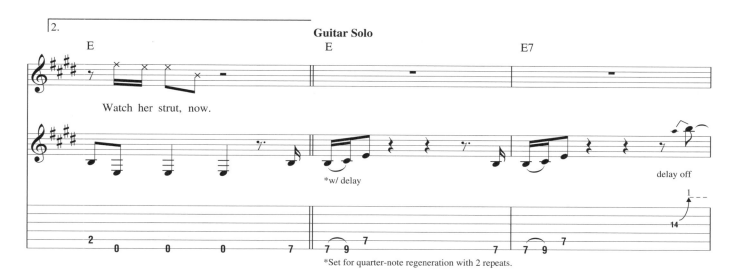

Watch her strut, now.

*w/ delay

delay off

*Set for quarter-note regeneration with 2 repeats.

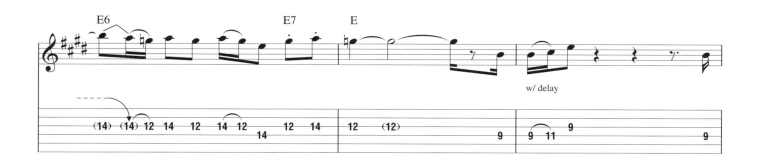

w/ delay

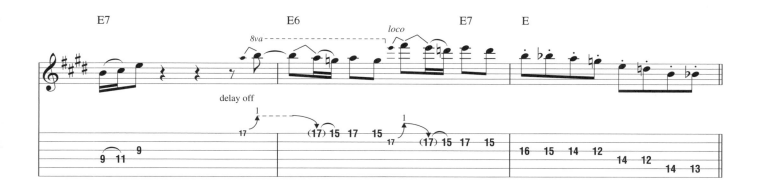

delay off

Love her strut.     Mm, _ hmm.     Love _ to,    love _ to     love _ to watch her

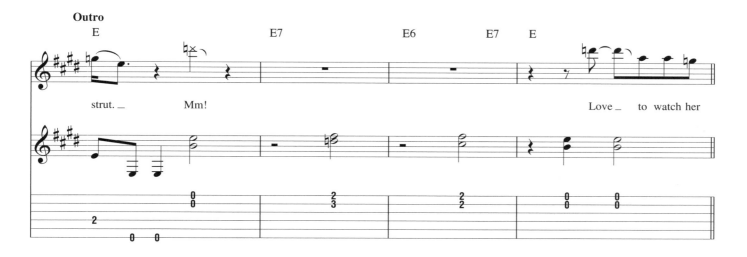

**Outro**

strut. _     Mm!        Love _ to watch her

*Repeat and fade*

w/ Voc. ad lib. on repeats

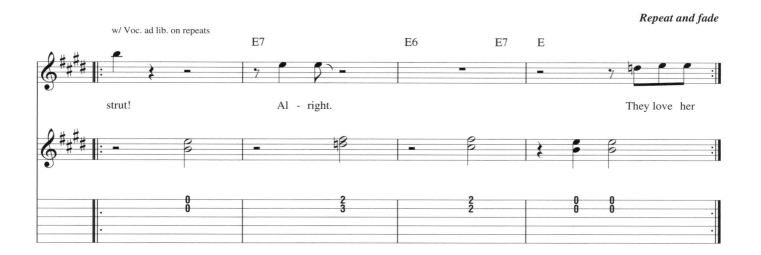

strut!     Al - right.        They love her

*Additional Lyrics*

2. Sometimes they'll want to leave her, just give up and leave her,
But they would never play that scene.
In spite of all her talking, once she starts in walking,
The lady will be all they ever dreamed.

*Chorus*   Oh, they'll love to watch her strut.
Oh, they'll kill to make the cut,
They love to watch her strut.

# Highway Star

Words and Music by Ritchie Blackmore, Ian Gillan, Roger Glover, Jon Lord and Ian Paice

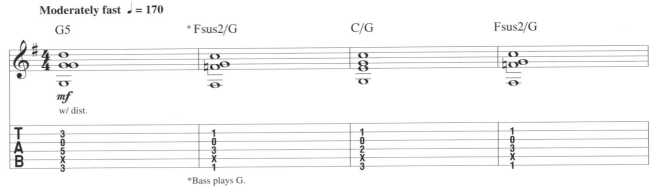

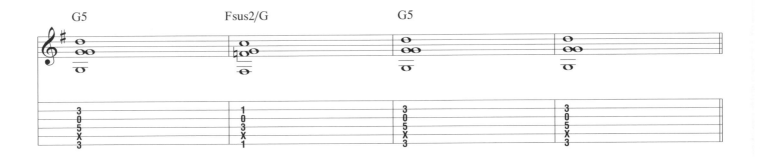

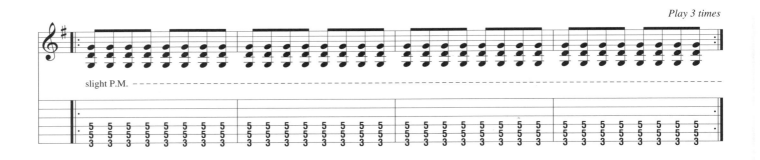

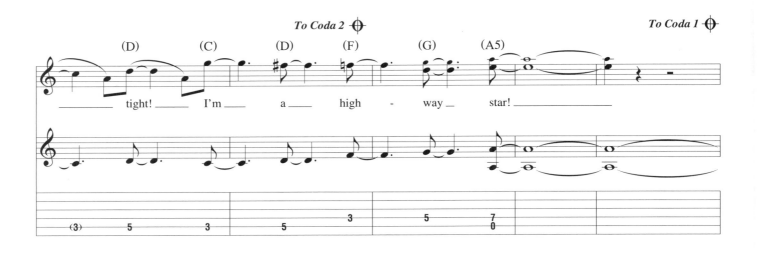

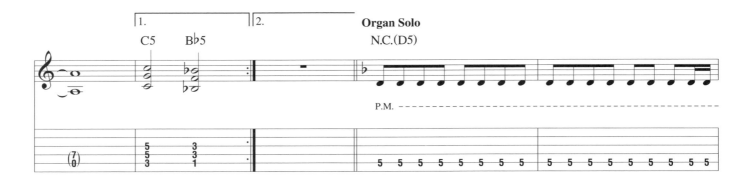

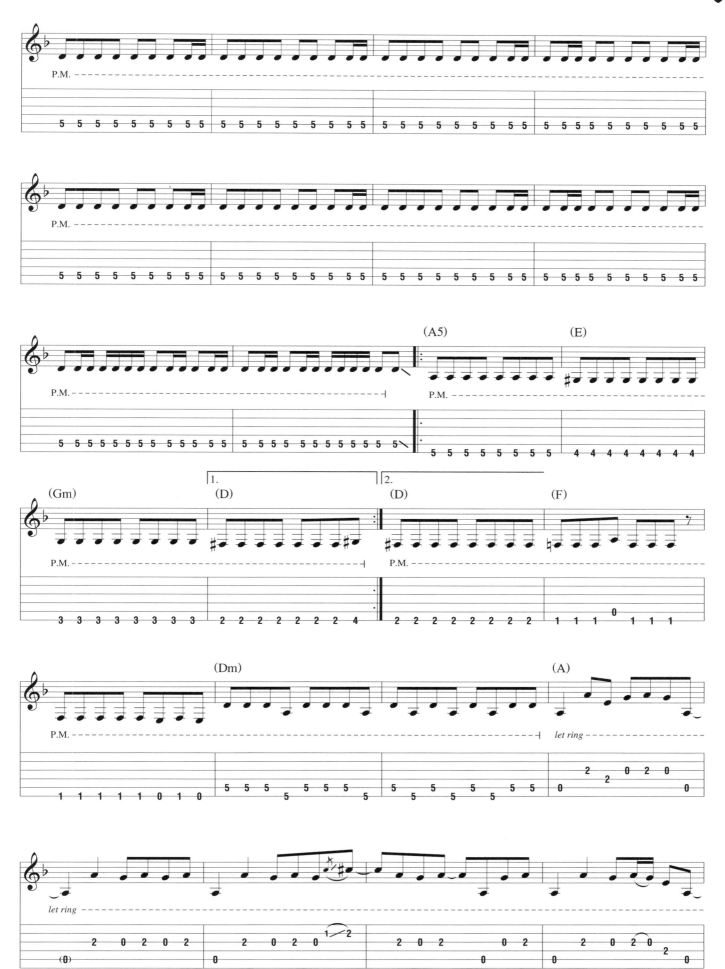

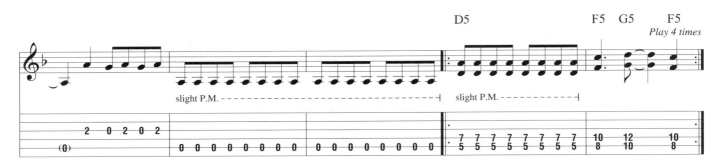

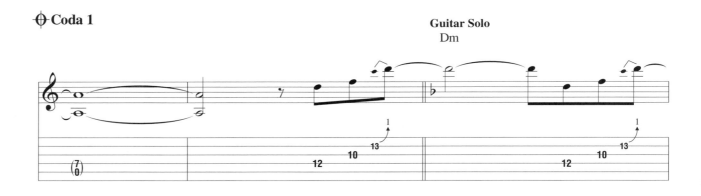

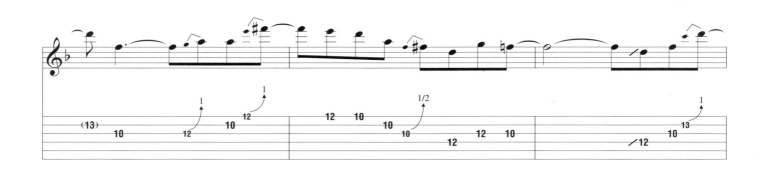

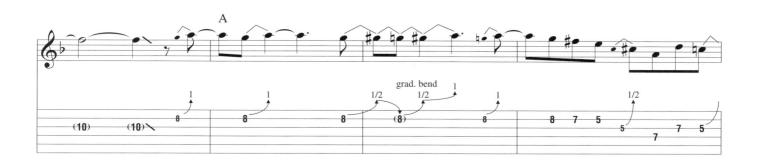

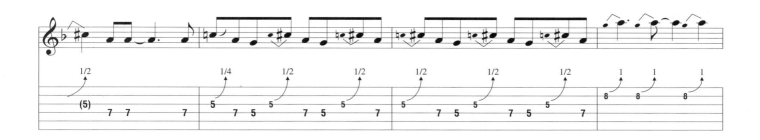

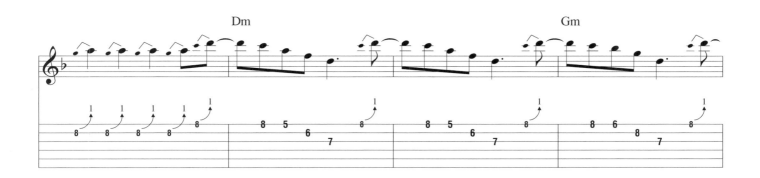

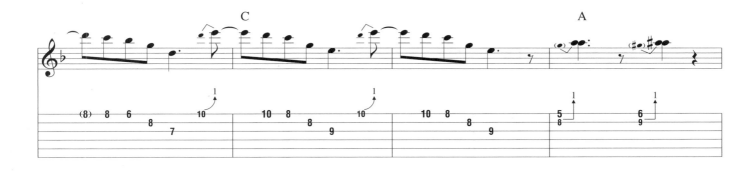

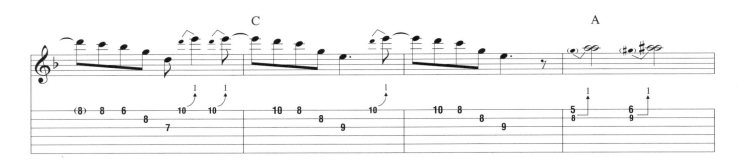

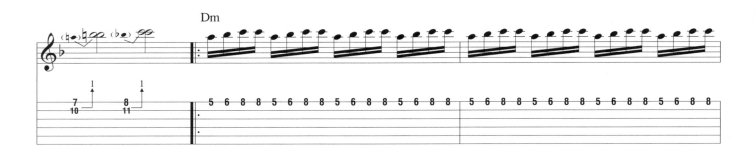

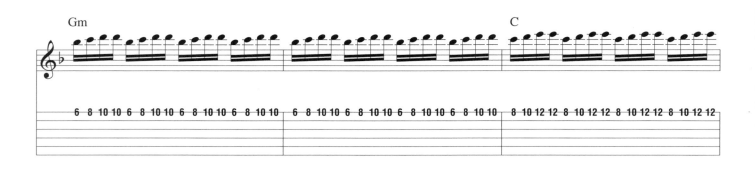

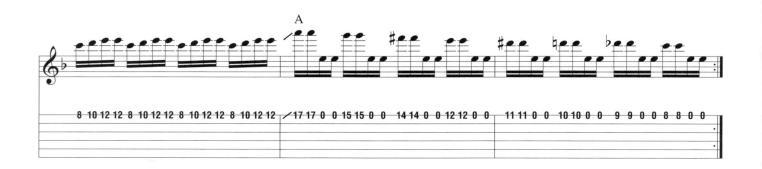

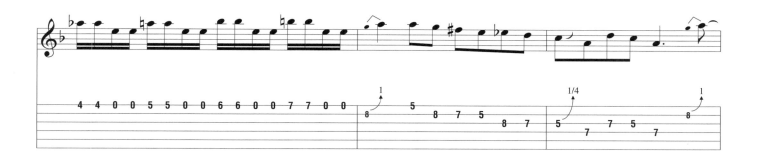

*D.S. al Coda 2*

**⊕ Coda 2**

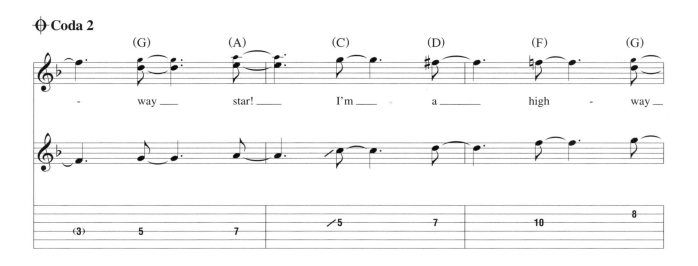

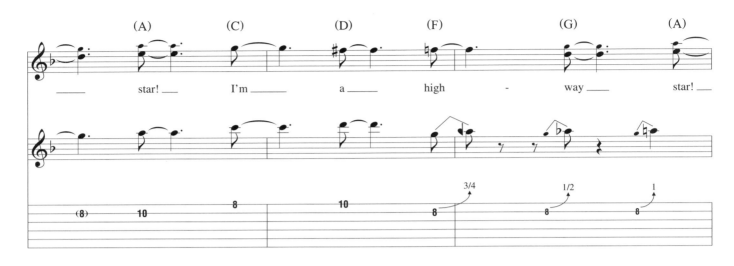

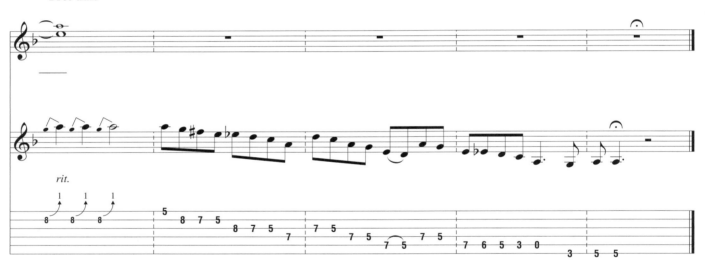

*Additional Lyrics*

2.  A nobody gonna take my girl, I gonna keep her to the end.
    A nobody gonna have my girl, she stays close on ev'ry bend.
    Ooh, she's a killin' machine. She got a ev'rything.
    Like a movin' mouth, body control and ev'rything.
    I love her! I need her! I see her!
    Yeah, she turns me on.
    All right! Hold tight!
    I'm a highway star!

3.  A nobody gonna take my head, I got speed inside my brain.
    A nobody gonna steal my head, now that I'm on the road again.
    Ooh, I'm in heaven again, I got a ev'rything.
    Like a movin' ground, an open road and ev'rything.
    I love her! I need her! I feel it!
    Eight cylinders, all mine!
    All right! Hold tight!
    I'm a highway star!

# I Won't Back Down

Words and Music by Tom Petty and Jeff Lynne

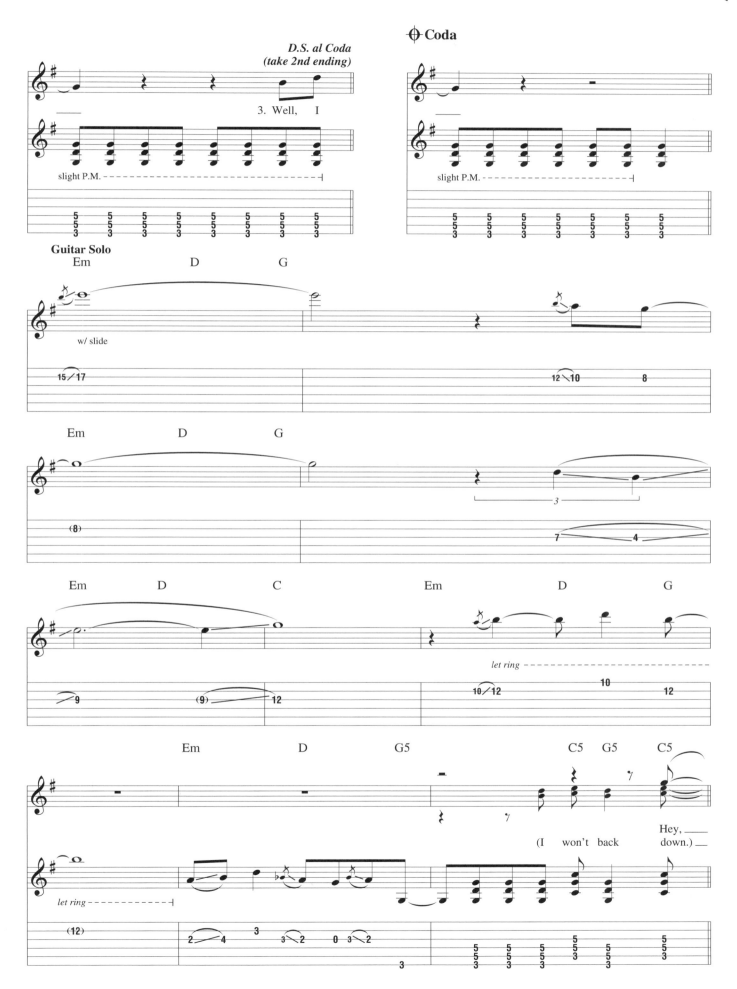

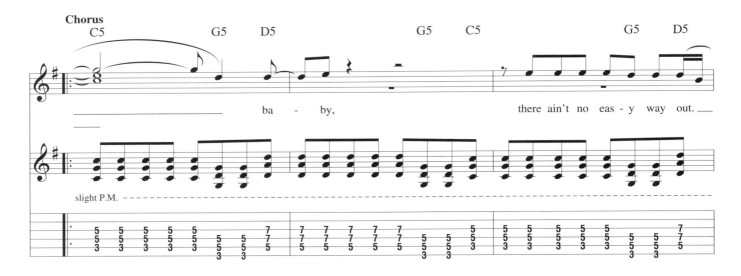

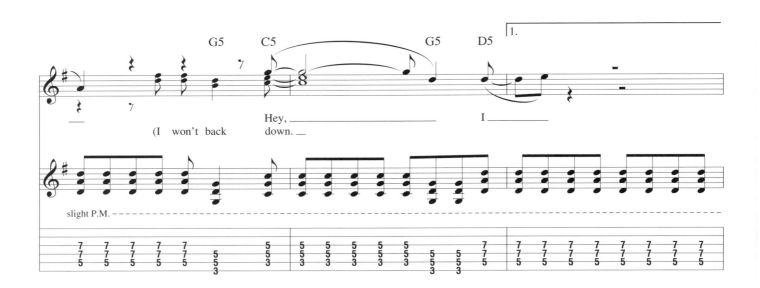

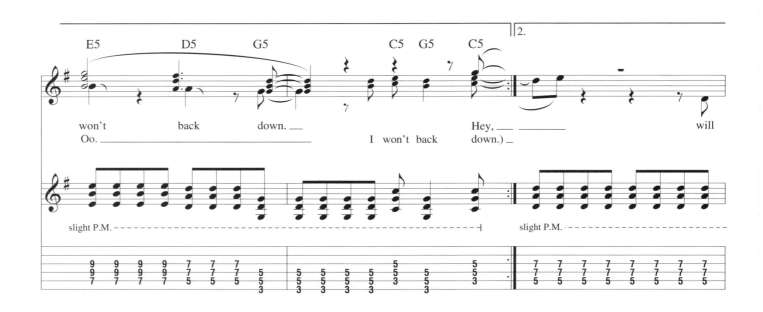

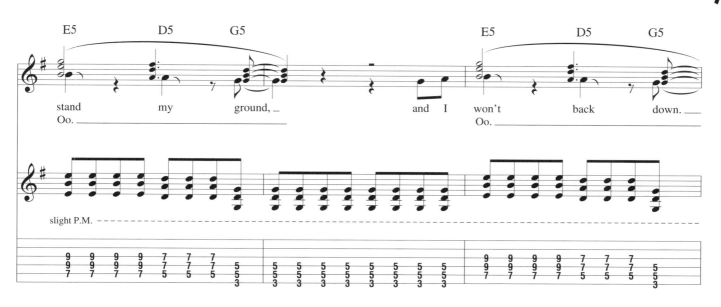

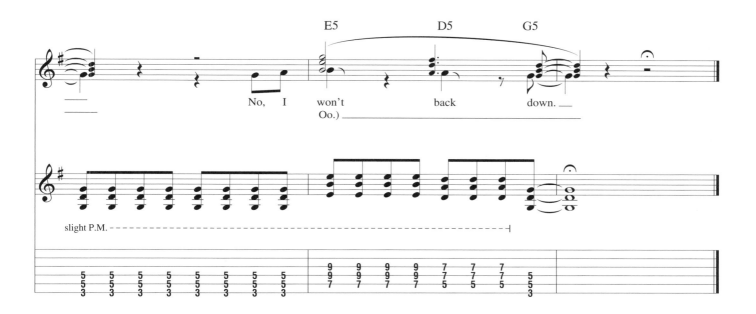

*Additional Lyrics*

2. No, I'll stand my ground.
   Won't be turned around.
   And I'll keep this world from draggin' me down,
   Gonna stand my ground.
   And I won't back down.

3. Well, I know what's right.
   I got just one life
   In a world that keeps on pushin' me around.
   But I'll stand my ground,
   And I won't back down.

# Highway to Hell

Words and Music by Angus Young,
Malcolm Young and Bon Scott

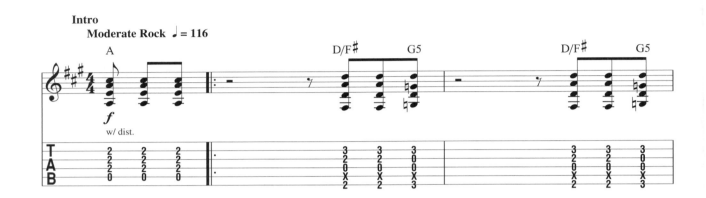

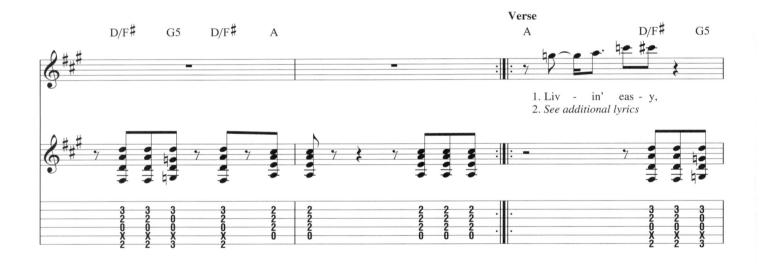

1. Liv - in' eas - y,
2. *See additional lyrics*

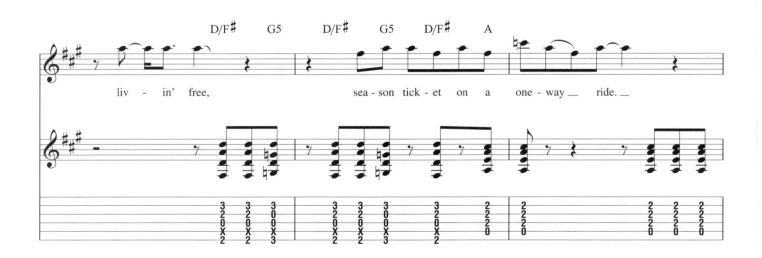

liv - in' free,        sea - son tick - et on a   one - way ___ ride. ___

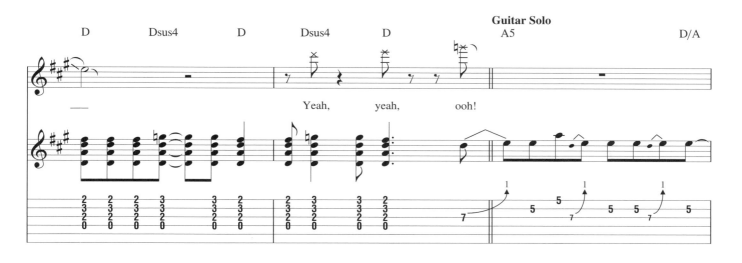

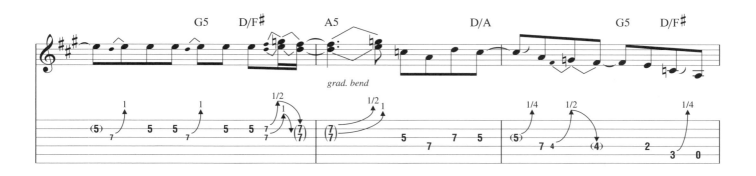

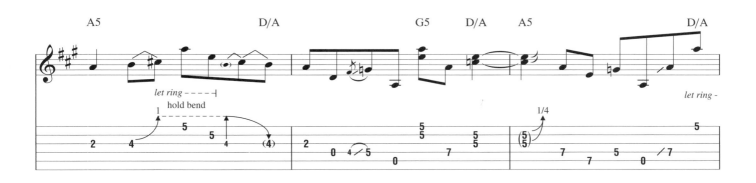

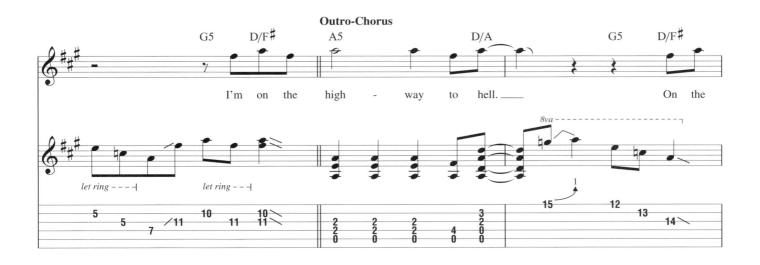

**Free time**

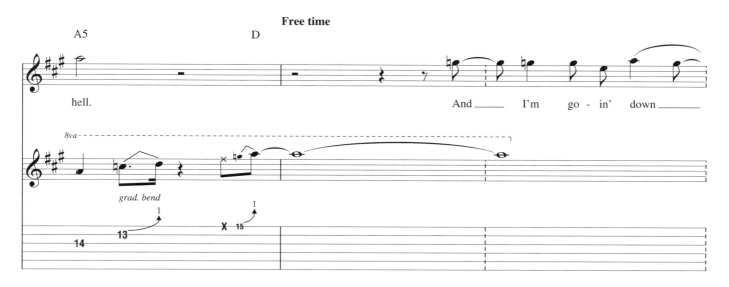

hell.                    And ____ I'm go-in' down ____

all _____ the     way. ____

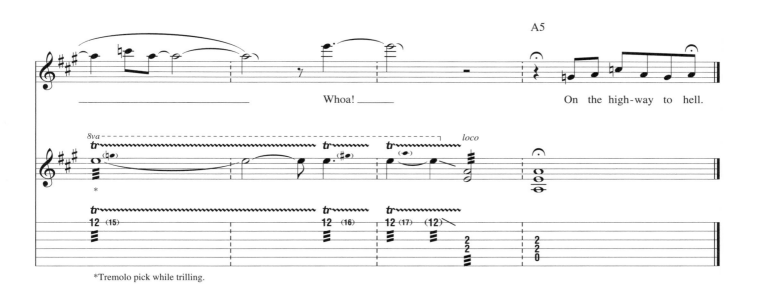

_____ Whoa! ____                    On the high-way to hell.

*Tremolo pick while trilling.

*Additional Lyrics*

2. No stop signs, speed limit, nobody's gonna slow me down.
   Like a wheel, gonna spin it, nobody's gonna mess me around.
   Hey Satan, pay'n' my dues, playin' in a rockin' band.
   Hey mama, look at me, I'm on my way to the promised land. Whoa!

*Chorus*  I'm on the highway to hell. Highway to hell.
          I'm on the highway to hell. Highway to hell.
          Mm. Don't stop me. Yeah, yeah, ooh!

# I Can't Explain

Words and Music by Peter Townshend

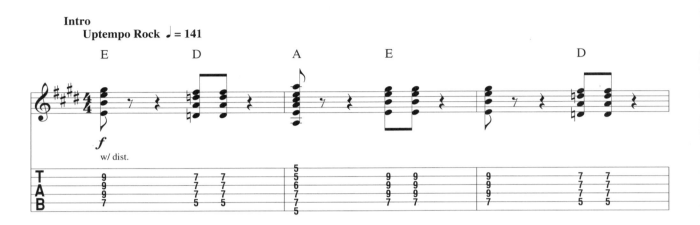

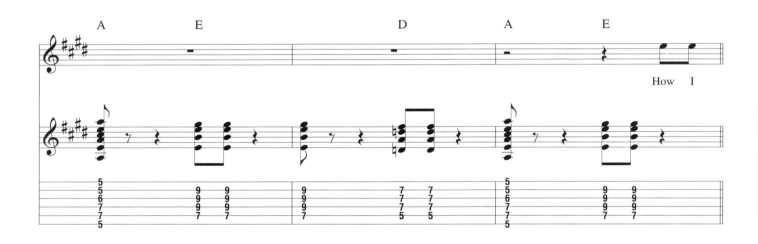

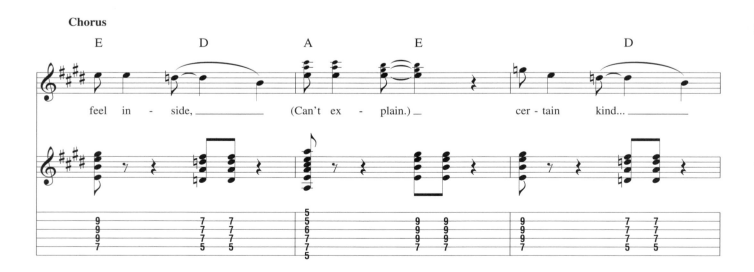

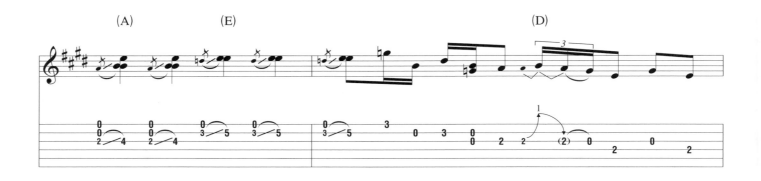

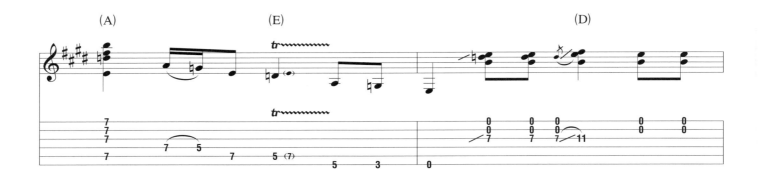

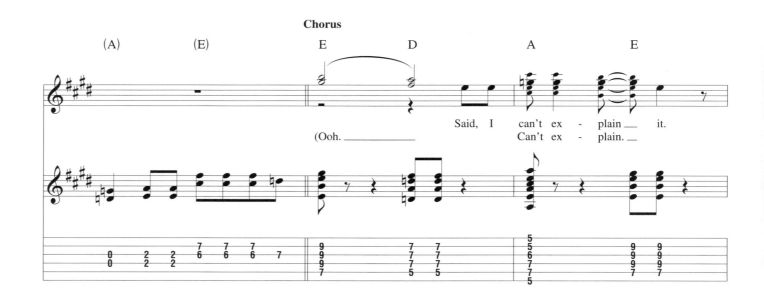

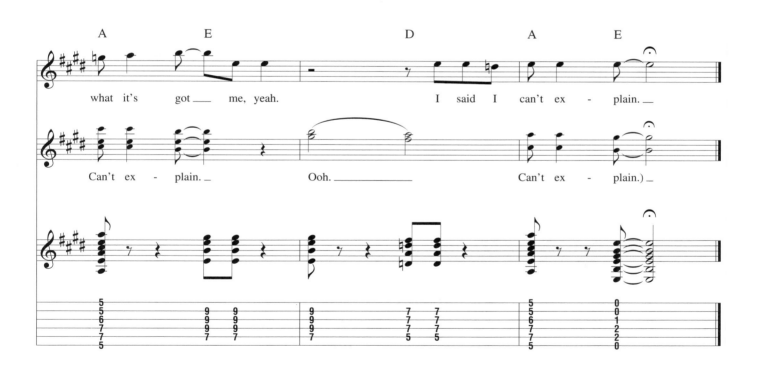

*Additional Lyrics*

2. Dizzy in the head, and I feel bad.
   The things you said got me real mad.
   I'm gettin' funny dreams again and again.
   I know what it means, but...

# Performance Notes

## Aqualung (page 6)

Jethro Tull (a band, not a person), one of the British progressive rock giants of the 1970s, continues to make their unique brand of art-rock. Tull's sound mixes classical, rock, and blues influences with a Celtic folk twist. From the 1971 album of the same name, "Aqualung" features the electric riffing of Martin Barre and the acoustic strumming of Ian Anderson. Both parts are covered on our arrangement, so you can wear both musical hats in one song (but don't take your hands off the guitar to switch hats).

"Capo III" isn't the name of a medieval Pope — it refers to the bar device you clamp on the fretboard to raise the pitch of all the strings. Put it on the third fret, and the end (or the "head") of the fretboard is III. The capo can be bought at any music store or, in desperate times, made from a pencil and a rubber band!

When you put on a capo, reality changes. The fret after the capo becomes fret 1, and it's best to think of all chords accordingly. On the sheet music, the chord symbols in parentheses (E) are in capo reality, and the ones listed above them reside in the parallel universe you just left behind.

The electric intro and verse are pretty well spelled out in the sheet music — check the Notation Legend for *vibrato, slides,* and *staccato* notes.

The chorus is *strummed,* which means that your picking hand is in constant motion, but not hitting the strings every time. Try holding down one chord and just strumming across the strings, "down–up–down–up–down–up–down–up." Keep repeating until you're in a steady rhythm, then try a new pattern: miss the strings on the first upstroke, so you're going "down, down–up–down–up–down–up" for every measure. That's the main strum pattern. When it kicks in, strum over those *muffled strings* (see the Guitar Notation Legend) for a "chick-a-chick-a" sound.

On you go to the interlude and guitar solo, where Barre follows the chord changes with licks full of slides, hammer-ons and pull-offs, vibrato, and bending — all explained in the handy Notation Legend.

## Authority Song (page 21)

On 1983's swaggering *Uh-Huh,* John Cougar Mellencamp, previously known as John Cougar, both perfected his infectious brand of heartland rock and brought back his surname. The third single from that album, the defiant "Authority Song," is Mellencamp's answer to the 1950s classic "I Fought the Law."

The song starts with a *pickup measure,* one that has fewer beats than a bar of the given meter. In this case, the first note, A, starts on the "and" of beat 3.

You may already know some songs in *drop D tuning,* in which the 6th string is tuned down, from E to D. But to play "Authority Song," you'll need to tune both your 6th and 1st strings down to D, for double *drop D tuning* (low to high: D–A–F–G–B–D).

The intro is filled with attitudinal half-step bends, from C♯ to D. In playing these bends, use your 3rd finger and push the string toward the floor in the specified rhythm. Make sure the pitch of the note to which you've bent matches that of the proceeding open D string or you'll sound pretty bad.

The verse and chorus are built from killer riffs that incorporate chunky three-note chords with a single-note move that is a staple of blues and rock, simply including both the minor 3rd (F) and the major 3rd (F♯). Play those two notes with your 2nd and 3rd fingers, respectively. One advantage of the song's tuning is that it allows for one-finger power chords to be played on strings 6 through 4. For example, whenever you see that G5 chord, just grab it with a 3rd-finger barre on the bottom three strings.

In the first several bars of the solo, the open E string is used as a drone for a great ringing sound. At the end of its eighth bar, the solo ventures up to 10th position, where maximum mileage is obtained from a single bend in various iterations. Until the end of the solo, keep your 3rd finger on the 12th-fret G and your 1st finger on the 10th-fret A. This time, bend the G toward the ceiling, making sure that you nail the note A. You'll know you're out of tune if you hear a pulsing sound when you play the bent note and the 10th-fret A together.

# Bad Case of Loving You (page 30)

In the mid-1980s, the singer Robert Palmer became famous — less for his music than for his music videos, in which he was nattily dressed and surrounded by ensembles of leggy ladies. But some of Palmer's earlier work has more artistic merit. Case in point is 1979's "Bad Case of Loving You," which finds the singer in a soulful mode and features some great guitar work as well.

The intro is built from E5 and D5/E chords in conjunction with a cool single-note line that comes from one of the most common scales in rock and blues: E minor pentatonic (E–G–A–B–D). If you don't already know that scale, commit its spelling to memory immediately. One thing to look out for in the single-note line is a *quarter-step bend,* which you can create by pulling the string toward the floor just a hair, so that its pitch is slightly raised. This is an example of a true *blue note,* which in this instance, is the bent note splitting the difference between the notes G and G♯.

The chorus contains an example of *stop time.* In the first four measures, the expected rhythms are disrupted by an extensive amount of rests. This technique provides some welcome contrast in a song with little harmonic variation, so avoid the temptation to noodle here, as so many guitarists are inclined to do when faced with silence.

The interlude, guitar solo, and coda use notes from the E minor pentatonic scale, this time largely in 12th position — use your 1st finger to depress the 12th-fret notes and your 3rd finger for those on the 14th fret. Throughout, pay close attention to the intonation of those bends, if necessary using a target note. For example, if you're bending the 3rd string's 14th-fret A up a whole step, first play that string's 16th-fret B to use as a reference pitch.

# Ballroom Blitz (page 38)

In the 1970s, the genre of glam rock emerged, with its outrageously costumed, androgynous musicians and highly theatrical performances. One of the most prominent glam bands of the 1970s was the British outfit Sweet, featuring the tasty guitar work of Andy Scott, as can be heard on one of the group's greatest hits: 1973's "Ballroom Blitz."

It might be hard, but for the first 18 bars of the tune, play nothing. Containing just drums and verbal exchanges, this portion of the intro is a great example of building anticipation for a tune.

"Ballroom Blitz" is played with a *swing feel*. To cop it, wherever you see a pair of eighth notes, play the first note longer than the second (at about a 2:1 ratio between the two notes). It's almost like you're playing a dotted eighth note followed by a 16th. But be sure not to play these rhythms in a mechanical way. Strive for a loose feel, and play along with the original recording if you find that the swing is lost on you.

The last eight bars of the intro and the verse contain an essential blues and rock rhythm move: a *shuffle pattern*. The most basic version of a shuffle pattern alternates between a power chord and a 6th chord, but the intro's variation incorporates a 7th chord. To play the variation, keep your 1st finger anchored on the 7th-fret E throughout and either your 2nd or 3rd finger on the 9th-fret B. Then, use your 4th finger to play the 11th-fret C♯ and the 12th-fret D, all the while remembering to maintain the swing feel.

In the verse, you'll find that the first four measures feature the more basic shuffle pattern in 5th position. Use a similar fingering here: your 1st finger on the 5th-fret A, your 2nd or 3rd on the 7th-fret E, and your 4th on the 9th-fret F♯. The P.M. sign calls for *palm muting* — lightly rest the side of your pick hand on the strings near the bridge as you pick. Use just enough pressure to create a muffled sound, but be sure not to use so much that your pitch is raised.

# *Bang a Gong (Get It On)* (page 46)

Mark Bolan, a British singer, songwriter, and guitarist who helped fuel the glam rock movement actually preferred his music to be called "cosmic rock." In 1971 Bolan and his group T. Rex released the innuendo-filled song "Bang a Gong (Get It On)" and it became Bolan's biggest hit, as well as one of the era's most emblematic tunes.

"Bang a Gong (Get It On)" kicks off with a classic shuffle pattern in open position. Depress the 2nd-fret B and 4th-fret C♯ with your 1st and 3rd fingers, respectively, and play all the notes with slight palm muting. Beginning in bar 3 is a lean riff that appears throughout most of the song. Although this part is very simple to play, it's possible that the syncopated rhythm will throw you off, so pay close attention to where the notes fall. In bar 3, for instance, open-string stabs fall on the "and" of beat 1 and on beat 3. Another thing: Be sure to deaden the strings right after you play the notes, to achieve a funky feel.

After you get the intro down, the verse and chorus should fall right into place. The first verse uses the same syncopated open-string hits as the intro and has only two chords: E5 and A5. Use all downstrokes when strumming these chords, and be sure to deploy and release the palm mute as indicated, if needed taking things slowly to ensure coordination between your fret and pick hands.

The chorus adds two-note power chords on strings 6 and 5, G5 and A5. Play each one with your 1st and 3rd fingers on the 6th and 5th strings, respectively, and again, strum in consistent downstrokes.

The subsequent verses are basically played the same as the first, save for the substitution of an A7 chord for A5. Whenever you see this chord, keep an A7 grip — your 1st finger on the 2nd-fret E, your 2nd on the 2nd-fret C♯, and your 3rd on the 3rd-fret G, with a slight palm mute on beat 1 only.

At the outro is just a hint of soloing, four bars within the E minor pentatonic scale (E–G–A–B–D) in 12th position. Here, as indicated by the staccato marks (dots) surrounding a bunch of the noteheads, play the indicated notes short and detached.

# Changes *(page 62)*

In the late 1960s, with his group the Experience, Jimi Hendrix made some of rock's strangest and most exciting music. After Hendrix and the Experience went their separate ways, in mid-1969, Hendrix (sort of) returned to his roots with the blues-rock outfit Band of Gypsies. That group's signature song, "Changes," finds Hendrix stretching out and playing with fierce abandon.

"Changes" is played in standard tuning, but each string is tuned down a half step (low to high: Eb–Ab–Db–Gb–Bb–Eb). Hendrix and many other rock guitarists have used this tuning for a couple of different reasons: to better accommodate vocal ranges and to make the strings more agreeable to bending. If you're not playing along with the original recording, you're allowed to be lazy and play in standard. Another thing to note: Wherever you see this tuning, the music sounds a half step higher than written.

Most of what you need to play "Changes" can be found in the intro. Although the song is in the overall key of E major, the first four bars feel more like A major, with a single-note riff drawn from the A Mixolydian mode (A–B–C#–D–E–F#–G) and pitted against the open 5th and 6th strings. When you see the crescendo mark in bar 4, simply increase your volume via one of your guitar's knobs or a volume pedal.

One of the song's main riffs, later heard in the choruses, is found in bars 5–6 and repeats in the following two measures. This riff is in E minor pentatonic (E–G–A–B–D) and features a sort of *call-and-response* technique: In each measure, the notes on beats 1–3 make a call, while the notes on beat 4 respond with an answer. You'll notice that throughout the song Hendrix improvises a number of subtle variations on this part. So, first learn it exactly as Hendrix played it, then try making up some of your own variations on the spot.

Another of the main riffs, which forms the verses, is found in the last couple bars of the intro. Based in E major pentatonic (E–F#–G#–B–C#), this part provides a nice tonal contrast to the previous riff. Here, play all the 7th-fret notes with your 1st finger and all the 9th-fret notes with your 3rd. Again, the idea is that if you learn those two bars well, you can spin your own variations throughout the verses.

# Deuce *(page 57)*

With their trademark painted faces and flamboyant outfits, Kiss is hard rock's most visually identifiable group. The band, formed in New York in 1973, has been known to put on equally outrageous, theatrical concerts, filled with fire-breathing, blood-spitting, and other such antics. But Kiss's music, as you'll see in 1974's "Deuce," is fairly straightforward hard rock fare.

The intro to "Deuce" is filled with aggressive *double stops* — two-note chords. To smoothly play them, you'll want to use some efficient fingerings. Start with the first four measures. For the A5 chord, keep your 1st finger barred across strings 3 and 4 at the 14th fret, adding and removing the 16th-fret F# with your 3rd finger. For the F/A chord, barre strings 5–3 at the 10th fret, adding the 12th-fret A with your ring finger; shift that whole shape up two frets for the G/B chord.

The last two measures of the intro contain double stops from within the A minor pentatonic scale (A–C–D–E–G), implying an A minor chord. Depress all the 5th-fret notes with your 1st finger and all the 7th-fret notes with your 3rd. And play everything with considerable attitude.

Kicking off in A minor pentatonic, the guitar solo has a symbol that might be unfamiliar to you. In the fourth and eighth bars of the solo, the *tr* sign stands for *trill* — a rapid alternation of notes. Here, stop the 5th-fret C with your 1st finger, and for the duration of a dotted half note rapidly hammer on and pull off the 7th-fret D with your third finger, aiming for a smooth and even sound. (You can read more about hammer-ons and pull-offs in the Guitar Notation Legend.)

The outro contains a second solo, which is based on the A minor pentatonic scale way up in 17th position — depress the 17th-, 19th-, and 20th-fret notes with, respectively, your 1st, 3rd, and 4th fingers. Right before the fade begins are some *sextuplets* — that's six notes per beat. If you have trouble feeling this rhythm, just break things down and *subdivide*. Tap your foot in eighth notes rather than quarters, with three notes falling on each tap. While feeling the rhythm, don't forget to play the hammer-ons and pull-offs as smoothly as possible with your fret hand.

## Don't Ask Me No Questions (page 78)

Lynyrd Skynyrd is the quintessential southern rock band, known for their hard-driving songs and killer lead and rhythm guitar work. "Don't Ask Me No Questions" was released as a single for the group's sophomore album, *Second Helping.* The song failed to chart, but thanks to one of the album's other songs, "Sweet Home Alabama," Skynyrd secured their status as southern rock stars.

"Don't Ask Me No Questions" has a certain swagger due to the use of *chromatic chords* — chords outside of the key that in this case, lead into those within the key via a half-step shift. For instance, in the F♯5–G5 and C♯5–D5 moves in the first system, the F♯5 and C♯5 chords are chromatic. By the way, play all these two-note chords with your 1st finger on the lower note and your 3rd on the higher one.

Another thing that gives the guitar work an undeniable swagger is the way in which the chords are articulated. To recreate this effect, be precise with your rhythms; where you see rests, cut off the sound with your fret hand and/or your pick hand. Observe all the staccato markings, too, by cutting the given notes short. Another thing to be mindful of is the *pick-hand muting.* Wherever you see X-shaped noteheads, release the pressure on your fret hand such that a percussive or scratching sound is produced when you pick or strum the strings.

In the guitar solo you'll travel through multiple positions of the G minor pentatonic scale (G–B♭–C–D–F). Being aware of these shifts in advance will help you concentrate on playing with expression. The solo starts off with an upper "box" of the scale in 6th position, played with the 1st finger on the 6th fret and the 3rd finger on the 8th. In the second half of the third bar of the solo, the music shifts quickly down to position III of the scale — here play the 5th-fret notes with your 3rd finger and the 3rd-fret B♭ with your 1st — before shifting back up to the box on the "and" of beat 4, then back and forth a bit between the box and the 3rd position. Finally, the 12th bar of the solo moves up to the 15th position of the scale. Note in bars 14 and 15 of the solo some more chromatic coolness where a B natural connects the notes B♭ and C.

## Funk #49 (page 84)

Formed in Cleveland, Ohio in 1966, the James Gang never achieved the overall huge commercial success that they were striving for. They did, however, score a pretty big hit with "Funk #49" — as you might guess from the title, a song filled with all kinds of awesome funk-guitar parts.

The first two measures of the intro have some guitar work that might at first be a bit tricky, so take your time in learning this section. In fact, play super slowly if needed. But before you play anything, plant your 4th finger on the 8th-fret G; on the 3rd string, depress the 5th, 6th, and 7th frets with your 1st, 2nd, and 3rd fingers, respectively. Now you're ready to rock. With all three fingers still on the 3rd string, bend the note D up a whole step, to E. Keep that note held and pick the 8th-fret G. Then, pick the 3rd string and release the bend, pulling off to the 5th-fret C and bending that note up a step, to D, with your 1st finger.

In the next measure, begin by pre-bending the 7th-fret D up a step. Keep the note bent while releasing finger pressure for a muted sound. Pick the string, then fully fret the note and pick it again. Repeat this move, gradually releasing the bend over the first two beats while keeping things going in your pick hand. Finally, on beat 4 of bar 2, play the 7th-fret notes with your 3rd finger and the 6th-fret notes with your 2nd, sort of inadvertently sounding the open B and G strings with your 2nd finger as you pull off from the 6th fret notes.

Much of the song has a classic funk guitar pattern featuring just two chords: A7 and D. For the A7 chord, barre strings 2–4 at the 5th fret with your 1st finger and hammer on the 6th-fret C♯ with your 2nd finger; for D, barre the 7th-fret notes with your first finger, hammering on the 8th- and 9th-fret notes with, respectively, your 2nd and 3rd fingers. Where indicated with X noteheads, remember to release fret-hand pressure for that cool muffled sound. Also, throughout the rhythmic passages, use *pendulum strumming:* Keep your pick hand moving in continuous up-and-down 16th notes, striking the strings only as needed.

# Her Strut *(page 88)*

Although Bob Seger has long been one of America's most prominent heartland rockers, he's only had one #1 album to date, 1980's *Against the Wind,* recorded with the Silver Bullet Band. From that album comes "Her Strut," a crunchy, rocking number reported to have been inspired by actress Jane Fonda's moves in the 1968 sci-fi flick *Barbarella.*

The song is in rock tuning, which is standard tuning down a half step (E♭–A♭–D♭–G♭–B♭–E♭). For more on rock tuning, see "Changes." Unless you plan to play along with the original recording, this tuning is optional.

The intro starts off simply enough with an open-position E5 chord decorated at the end of bar 2 by a trill. Use whatever fret-hand finger is most comfortable to play the trill, and for more on the technique, refer to the notes for "Deuce." At the end of bar 4, note that the single-note line contains both the minor 3rd (G) and the major (G♯), a classic move similar to one seen in "Authority Song."

The next several bars have another cool riff in which a descending line on each beat 1 (E–D–C♯) is drawn from the E Mixolydian mode (E–F♯–G♯–A–B–C♯–D) and pitted against the open 6th string, as well as that minor-major move. Play the riff in 2nd position, with your 1st finger on the 2nd-fret notes, your 4th on the 5th-fret D, and your 3rd on the 4th-fret C♯. Pick everything with a bit of swagger. This part continues into the verse; heads up on the bluesy quarter-note bend at the end of the eighth bar of that section.

The guitar solo makes use of a *delay pedal,* for those unfamiliar, that's a device that records a sound and plays it back after a desired amount of time and repeats it a specified amount of times. In this case, you should set your delay pedal to repeat in quarter notes. To do so, use a delay time of 500 milliseconds, and set the regeneration so that the pedal provides two repeats. When you play through the music, be sure to turn the pedal on and off as indicated.

As for the pitch content of the solo, after a couple of bars, the solo hits the 12th position of the E minor pentatonic scale (E–G–A–B–D) before shifting down to hint at E major pentatonic (E–F♯–G♯–B–C♯) beginning at the very end of bar 4. At the end of the 6th bar, the solo shifts up to a 15th-position box of the E minor pentatonic scale before hitting the E blues scale (E–G–A–B♭–B–D) in 12th position in the final measure. In that last measure, be sure to cut the eighth notes short as indicated by the staccato marks.

# *Highway Star* (page 94)

The title track from Deep Purple's 1972 album, "Highway Star" is one of the band's most killer cuts with its fast-paced, classically inspired organ and guitar solos. It's also considered to have provided the blueprint for the speed metal style of such later groups as Motörhead and Metallica.

The chord work in "Highway Star" should be straightforward enough, mostly three-note power chords. Although not shown in the notation, some of the intro's chords might be easiest to play with some thumb-fretting. For the G5 and Fsus2/G chords, wrap your thumb around the neck to fret the lowest notes. Meanwhile, use your 3rd finger both to fret the 4th-string note and (with the fingertip) mute the 5th string.

Richie Blackmore's solo, in which the guitarist went for a "Bach sound," is considered by many to be one of the greatest ever recorded in rock and roll. The first 16 bars are more blues than Bach, though. Atop a Dm chord, bars 1–8 are based on the D minor pentatonic scale (D–F–G–A–C) in 10th position; over an A chord, bars 9–16 are drawn from the A minor pentatonic scale (A–C–D–E–G) in 5th position. These 16 measures should be easy enough to play, just make sure to pay close attention to your intonation on the many bends.

Beginning in bar 17 of the solo, a more classical approach is seen. Until the 32nd bar, Blackmore thinks not in terms of scales but *arpeggios* (chords played one night at a time). In bar 17, for instance, he outlines a Dm triad (D–F–A) in descending fashion; in bar 19 he does the same with a 2nd-inversion G minor triad (5th in the bass, D–G–B♭) and in bar 21 with a 1st-inversion C major triad (3rd in the bass, E–G–C). Meanwhile, Blackmore flanks these arpeggios with pre-bent unison bends. Again, pay close attention to these bends and try to train your muscle memory to know the exact distance you need to bend a string before you pick it. And in each unison bend, make sure that you don't hear any pulsating between the two adjacent notes.

In bar 33, Blackmore returns to a *scalar* (pertaining to a scale) approach, travelling up D natural minor (D–E–F–G–A–B♭–C) on the 1st string. Use alternate picking here, and your 1st, 2nd, and 4th fingers on the three notes of each measure, lowest to highest. Beginning in bar 39 is another classical approach in which Blackmore uses the open high E string as a *pedal tone* (constant note) against different fretted notes on that string. Note that beginning in 40, the notes are from the *chromatic scale,* which contains all 12 notes. Again, use alternate picking, taking things slowly at first to ensure coordination between your pick and fret hands.

# *Highway to Hell* (page 108)

The tandem guitar attack of Aussie brothers Angus Young and Malcolm Young is one of the most potent in rock. From AC/DC's sixth album, *Highway to Hell* (1979), the title track has some of the guitarists' best work, with Malcolm playing pulverizing power chords and Angus laying down stinging leads.

A typical AC/DC song makes the most out of a few simple grips, and containing variations on just four basic chords — A, D, G, and E. "Highway to Hell" is no exception. One thing that makes the rhythm parts of "Highway to Hell" so cool is the judicious use of space. So make sure that not a sound emanates from your guitar where you see a rest. Remember, what you *don't* play is as important as what you do. A word on fingering: For the D/F♯ chord, you might try wrapping your thumb around the neck to fret the lowest note, F♯.

Played mostly in the 5th position of the A minor pentatonic scale (A–C–D–E–G), the guitar solo is fairly straightforward. It does, though, have some bends that might at first be tricky to execute. At the end of the solo's second bar is a double-stop move in which each note is bent to a different degree. To play this bend, barre strings 2–3 with your ring finger, if necessary using target notes: the 2nd string's 8th-fret G and the 3rd string's 9th-fret E. Practice bending and releasing these notes very slowly, making sure that everything sounds in tune.

For the country-inflected bend in the solo's fifth bar, a little preplanning will help you sound smooth. Before you play anything, barre strings 1 and 2 with your 4th finger at the 5th fret. Bend the 4th-fret C with your 3rd finger, reinforced by your 1st and 2nd strings, and keep the bend held while you play the pre-fingered notes on the 1st and 2nd strings.

Beginning in bar 7, the indication P.S. calls for a *pick scrape*. Simply slide your pick down strings 4 and 5 for the specified duration. In the last several bars of the section, each set of three slanted parallel lines stands for *tremolo picking*. Using alternating strokes, pick the indicated note(s) as quickly and evenly as possible. Practice tremolo picking on its own before adding the fret-hand trills indicated in the notation.

# I Can't Explain *(page 114)*

Awesome songwriter, expert guitar decimator, choreographer of the windmill guitar stroke, and inventor of the rock opera, Pete Townshend is also one of rock's finest rhythm guitarists. Not only that, Townshend is a great soloist, as can be heard on "I Can't Explain," the Who's first single, from 1965.

"I Can't Explain" is played mostly from 5th- and 6th-string-rooted chords, that is, those whose roots, or lowest notes, are on the 5th and 6th strings. To play the 5th-string rooted chords (E and D), fret the lowest note with your 1st finger and the top three notes with a 1st-finger barre. For the 6th-string rooted chords (A and B), use a 1st-finger barre across all six strings and your 3rd, 4th, and 2nd fingers, on the 5th, 4th, and 3rd strings, respectively. Strum everything forcefully, using lots of downstrokes, and be mindful of the extensive rests throughout (also see the notes for "Highway to Hell").

To play Townshend's second guitar solo, it's best to use *hybrid picking*. In the first measure of the solo, for example, pick the 2nd-fret E with your guitar pick and the 3rd-fret D with your middle finger. Beginning in the second bar's second half, pick the 7th-fret E with your guitar pick, the 7th-fret D with your middle finger, and the 7th-fret B with your ring finger. Experiment with a combination of flesh and nail on the fingerpicked notes, to find the best tone for you, and make sure that the flatpicked and fingerpicked notes sound at equal volume.

Another thing to note in this solo is the use of *quarter-note triplets* — three quarter notes in the space normally occupied by two, indicated by a bracketed 3 — in the second and third measures. This type of rhythm can be rather difficult to feel when the rest of the band is playing straight quarter notes, but if you break things down you should be okay. Here's how to do so: Try counting eighth-note triplets on each beat: "trip-uh-let, trip-uh-let," and so on. In the span of two beats, a quarter note will then fall on the first "trip," the first "let," and the second "uh." If this rhythm is giving you trouble, count and practice it extremely slowly, using just one note, until you feel it naturally. Then you'll be all set to play the rhythm in context.

# I Won't Back Down *(page 103)*

Singer-songwriter-guitarist Tom Petty has long been celebrated for his no-nonsense, rootsy brand of rock. "I Won't Back Down," the defiant first single from the 1989 album *Full Moon Fever,* finds Petty in top form, singing and playing alongside former Beatle George Harrison.

Made exclusively of three-note power chords rooted on strings 5 and 6, the rhythm work in "I Won't Back Down" shouldn't provide too many problems for you. The song's moderate tempo of 112 beats per minute will allow you to strum using downstrokes exclusively. One thing to look out for, though, is that certain chords are anticipated by an eighth note. For example, the expected position of the song's first G5 chord would be squarely on beat 1 of bar 2. The chord, however, arrives a little early, on the "and" of beat 4 in bar 1.

The guitar solo is played with a *slide* — a glass or metal tube placed on a fret-hand finger to stop the notes. If you're new to slide playing, get one and place it on your fret hand's 3rd finger. Before tackling the solo, try playing some random notes on your guitar. As opposed to conventional fretting, you'll want to place the slide directly over the fretwire of the desired note. Press down lightly, so that there's no contact between the strings and the fret, which would result in an unwanted buzz.

Using a slide can cause open strings to ring out inadvertently, so use lots of muting when playing slide. For example, when playing the solo's first few notes, rest the palm of your fret hand on the unplayed bottom strings, and rest your ring and/or pinky finger on the 1st string, to prevent it from sounding.

## Jungle Love (page 137)

In the late 1960s Steve Miller was a prominent Bay Area blues-rocker and in the 1970s he became a pop star. From that second period is "Jungle Love," included on 1977's *Book of Dreams,* a hit album that has now gone platinum three times.

"Jungle Love" is played in open A tuning (low to high: E–A–E–A–C♯–E). To get into open A, tune your 4th, 3rd, and 2nd strings up a step, from G, D, and B, respectively. Open A puts quite a bit of additional tension on the neck, so alternatively you could play in the slacker tuning of open G (D–G–D–G–B–D). Tune your 6th, 5th, and 1st strings down a step, from E, A, and E, respectively. Whatever tuning you use, be sure to play around in it — you might find yourself coming up with some cool new riffs.

The riffs in "Jungle Love" will be a bit easier to play than they look, so long as you seek out logical fingerings, some of which might not be apparent from the tab. For instance, in the first bar of the verse, maintain a barre across strings 1 through 5 at the 7th fret for the first three beats; for the A chord, play the 8th-fret A and the 9th-fret C♯ with, respectively, your 2nd and 3rd fingers. At the end of the measure, barre the D5 chord with your first finger, then, in the second bar of the verse, second half, play the 5th-fret G with your 3rd finger and the 5th-fret F♯ with your 4th. Play the next two chord grips with your 2nd finger on the 4th string and your 1st finger on the 2nd string.

Although most of the song is in the key of E major, the chorus modulates to the key of F♯ minor. This change in tonality helps maintain the listener's interest.

Fill 2 contains what are known as *natural harmonics* — notes that result when a string is divided at various locations. Natural harmonics are most easily found at the 12th, 7th, and 5th frets. To play the harmonics shown here, lightly barre your 3rd finger above the 7th fret, and let all the notes, which form an E major arpeggio, ring together as you pick them. You'll know that you're playing the harmonics properly if you hear a lovely, chimelike sound.

## La Grange (page 142)

Billy F. Gibbons is an actor, a car modifier, and the holder of nine U.S. patents. But he's best know as the guitarist of ZZ Top, the four-decade-old American blues-rock trio. Gibbons is one of the most revered instrumentalists in blues rock, and in checking out "La Grange," from 1973's *Tres Hombres,* it's easy to see why.

"La Grange" is all about the shuffle. Most of the song is centered around the rhythmic pattern introduced in the first two measures. In learning the tune, it might be a good idea to isolate these measures. Count in triplets — "One-uh-let, two-uh-let, three-uh-let, four-uh-let" — and be mindful of where the chord strums fall in relation to the count. For example, in bar 1 there's a chord on the "let" of every beat. Practice counting and playing these two bars obsessively, until you've got that mean swing feel down cold. Also, heads up on the bluesy quarter-step bend that occurs here and there: Grab the 5th-fret C with your 4th finger and nudge the string slightly toward the floor.

Although "La Grange" has a main key of A major, when the solo arrives the music is transposed to the key of C, for a nice tonal contrast. Much of the solo is based on the C minor pentatonic scale (C–E♭–F–G–B♭) in 11th position — look out for all the eighth-note triplets (three spaced evenly in a beat). Where you see the indication "w/ pick & finger," pick the given lower notes with your pick and the higher ones with your middle finger.

In the outro-guitar solo you'll find a bunch of *pinch harmonics,* indicated as "P.H." in the notation. To play a pinch harmonic, place your pick such that your thumb grazes a string when you pick a note, resulting in the sounding of a squealing harmonic. Although the transcription indicates the note names of the harmonics, it's unlikely that Gibbons was thinking about pitch in those instances, so just go for that squealing sound without worrying too much about the note name.

# Lay Down Sally *(page 152)*

From 1977's *Slow Hand,* "Lay Down Sally" is one of Eric Clapton's greatest pop hits. With a rhythm section comprised of American country musicians, the song was also a crossover hit, going to #26 on the C&W charts in 1978. And with its simple structure and infectious riffing, the song is now a favorite of bar-band guitarists everywhere.

Conveniently for you, most of the riffing for the entire song is found in the first four measures. Throughout the tune, every accompaniment part that Clapton plays is based on the music seen here. So, in learning "Lay Down Sally," first isolate these bars. Play the 2nd-, 4th-, and 5th-fret notes with your 1st, 3rd, and 4th fingers, respectively. Palm mute everything except for the selected notes in bar 2, where you'll let the open G string ring out against notes from the A Mixolydian mode (A–B–C♯–D–E–F♯–G) on string 4. After you learn the intro, see if you can riff along with the entire original recording without looking at the music, as you go along improvising subtle variations like Clapton did.

Clapton's solo lies mostly within the A minor pentatonic scale (A–C–D–E–G) in 5th position, with several shifts to extended positions of the scale. Here's how to finger them: At the end of bar 12, play the 5th-fret C with your 3rd finger and after sliding up to the 9th-fret E, play the 8th-fret G with your 2nd finger. Then, at the end of the next bar, with your 3rd finger still on the 9th-fret E, slide down to the 7th-fret D and catch the 1st-fret C with your 1st finger, putting you back in 5th position.

In the 15th bar of the solo, the scale shifts in the opposite direction. After sliding to the 5th from the 7th fret with your 3rd finger, play the 3rd- and 5th-fret notes with your 1st and 3rd fingers, respectively. Once you've learned these new positions of the A minor pentatonic scale, try improvising your own solo on "Lay Down Sally," just as you did with the riffing.

# London Calling *(page 166)*

With their highly politicized lyrics, hard-edged sound, and experimental tendencies, the Clash were part of the first wave of British punk rock. The Clash's third album, 1979's *London Calling,* found the group borrowing from unlikely sources: jazz, reggae, rockabilly, and more. The title track has some particularly cool work from guitarists Joe Strummer and Mick Jones.

The rhythm guitar work in "London Calling" is rather economical; only four different chord positions are used in the entire song. Most are played on the top four strings, a smart strategy often employed in jazz and reggae that keeps the guitar out of the bass guitar's range, so the sound doesn't get all murky. You might've noticed that the first grip, fretted with fingers 3, 4, 2, and 1, lowest note to highest, is played from the intro until the seventh measure of the verse, while the chord symbols change. What the heck? The note played by the bass guitar is what's changing, which causes the same chord grip to transform in function.

Regarding the pick hand during these rhythm parts, play everything tight and staccato — think like a reggae guitarist, in other words. Strum the quarter-note passages all in downstrokes and the eighth-note sections in alternating strokes. Although it'd be cool to get those scratches on the "and" of beats 1 and 3 in there, you could omit them if you're too lazy to play them, as a typical reggae pattern only involves strums on 2 and 4.

As indicated in the notation, the solo contains a backwards guitar arranged for standard. You can recreate this with an inexpensive digital multi-effects unit, which will simulate a *backwards effect* — a sound that could only be created in the studio in 1979 when the song was recorded. Although the notes of the solo are stock, all from the E minor pentatonic scale (E–G–A–B–D), the phrasing is slightly eccentric, so be sure to follow the rhythms faithfully. Also, the bends in bar 7 might be a little tricky. Although the measure starts off with a single pre-bent note on the 3rd string, you'll want to pre-bend the 2nd string at the same time, because you'll be playing that latter string in a second. Try using a 1st-finger barre on the top strings to pre-bend the 12th-fret notes up a step, if needed, using the 14th-fret notes on strings 2 and 3 as reference. If that's too difficult, use your 3rd finger instead to fret the two-note bend.

# Oye Como Va (page 159)

In the late 1960s and early 1970s guitarist Carlos Santana became famous for his fiery brand of Latin rock, in which he fused together rock 'n' roll, salsa, and jazz rhythms with high-intensity blues. From the 1970 classic *Abraxas,* one of Santana's signature songs is a cover of the Tito Puente number "Oye Como Va," filled with great rhythm work and some pretty sick soloing.

"Oye Como Va" is basically a two-chord jam. The Am7–D9 progression seen in the first two measures of the verse serves as the foundation of most of the song. So in learning the tune you might first concentrate on these two measures, copping the cool Latin groove by nailing the syncopation — beginning in the second half of the first measure, each chord falls on the "and" of a beat.

Next try tackling Santana's lead. One thing that makes the guitarist's playing so expressive is his use of *dynamics.* For instance, in the intro he switches back and forth between *mf* (*mezzo-forte,* meaning "moderately loud") and *mp* (*mezzo-piano,* meaning "moderately soft"). Try throwing some of your own dynamics into the music as you see fit. Remember, if you always talked at the same volume level, you'd sound rather monotonous, so don't play that way, either.

As for the pitch content of the solos, Santana draws largely within the A minor pentatonic scale (A–C–D–E–G). Within the scale he tends to be conscious of chord tones. For instance, in his first solo he begins by outlining an Am7 chord (A–C–E–G). In navigating the D9, he often lands on the chord's 3rd, F♯. This note, by the way, is not in A minor pentatonic but is found in the A Dorian mode (A–B–C–D–E–F♯–G). At the end of the fourth bar of the solo, Santana does a backwards rake across the highest three notes of a D9 chord shape, that is, he picks the notes with a single upstroke. This sort of approach to soloing — thinking harmonically — can help you bust out of the pentatonic rut that many guitarists find themselves in.

# Peace of Mind (page 174)

Engineer and inventor Tom Scholz is best known as being the founder and guitarist of the rock band Boston. Purportedly, Scholz was a senior engineer at Polaroid when he wrote "Peace of Mind," a song rejecting the materialism of Baby Boomers in corporate jobs. From Boston's 1976 self-titled debut, the song has awesome rhythm and lead work from Scholz.

The intro's first several bars reveal a cool chordal technique. A 5th-string-rooted C♯m is reinforced with the chord's 5th (G♯) on string 6, making for an extra-thick C♯m/G♯ chord. You can use this sort of reinforcement on any chord with a 5th-string root, major or minor. Strum all the chords in alternating strokes, being sure to get that fret-hand muting in there. (For more on this type of muting, see the notes to "Don't Ask Me No Questions.")

Beginning at the end of bar 4 of the intro is an especially melodic lead line based on the C♯ natural minor scale (C♯–D♯–E–F♯–G♯–A–B). Here, use your 1st, 2nd, and 4th fingers to play, respectively, the 4th-, 6th-, and 7th-fret notes. Make sure to nail the rhythms; if needed, subdivide, feeling the music in eighth notes instead of quarters. Each 16th-note triplet — three evenly spaced 16ths, indicated with a bracketed three — will fall squarely on beat 3.

You might also want to subdivide in the guitar solo, which is filled with syncopated rhythms and sixteenth-note triplets. The solo is filled with notes that are bent with vibrato. This takes a bit of skill, so if the technique is new to you, begin slowly. Bend the string up a whole step, then release it just a hair, bend it back up, and repeat, gradually increasing the speed of the bending and releasing until you find yourself making a nice, singing sound. An additional tip: It might help to wrap your thumb around the neck when working on the bend-and-vibrato technique.

# Reeling in the Years (page 192)

Steely Dan has been host band to some of the world's greatest guitarists. Their debut album, *Can't Buy a Thrill,* was released in 1972 and made a big impression with this and other hit songs, which soon became FM radio staples. "Reeling in the Years" features one of rock's all-time great guitar solos, performed by Elliott Randall. The equally mesmerizing Jeff "Skunk" Baxter was also part of the guitar lineup.

Look to "Ballroom Blitz" for guidance on *swing feel.*

The intro solo is connoisseur material, beginning with a *chromatic pull-off* lick and *slide,* then *vibrato* on the high E string. (Tip: wiggle the string by pushing it upwards, so it doesn't come off the edge of the neck and make an ugly sound.) There's a half-step bend that you need to pull downwards, and a series of *hammers* and *pulls* that involve three fingers. Lots of *slides* and *grace notes* add to the madness, all based on A *Mixolydian mode* (consult your local jazz expert if you want to learn more on that).

The verse is a breath of fresh air: barre the two highest strings on fret 5, and move notes around in relation to that. Let the strings ring throughout.

In the chorus, start by holding the bottom of a G chord, and fret notes around that. On the A chord, bar the chord at fret 2 and add fingers on frets 3 and 4. Then come the fills, more tasty techniques to look up in the Notation Legend.

Ah, the classic interlude. Hint: when you play over the A chord, you can hold a barre over the D, G, and B strings — until the second ending, where you must pull off three notes at lightning speed.

The guitar solo can't be dissected into words, but consider that there's a lot of position shifting involved. The outro solo is centered at fifth fret, and a barre across the two highest strings will come in handy for lots of those licks — especially the bending at the fadeout. Godspeed!

# Revolution (page 202)

"Revolution" has a rare spot in the Beatles catalog as being one of the group's only overtly political songs. It was released in a few different versions — a slow one, as heard on *The Beatles (White Album)* from 1968 and a faster, electrified one heard that same year as the B side of the "Hey Jude" single. The arrangement here is of the more rocking version.

"Revolution" is shown here with a *capo* — a clamping device that raises the pitch of the open strings — at the 2nd fret. Because of this, the music sounds a whole step higher than written. And because the capoed fret is "0" in the transcription, each tab number is two frets lower than the one actually being played. Unless you're jamming along with the original recording, though, the capo is optional.

"Revolution" is played with a swing or triplet feel, so throughout it might be a good idea to count "One-uh-let, two-uh-let, three-uh-let, four-uh-let," and so on. For more on the swing feel, see the notes to "Ballroom Blitz."

The song kicks off with a classic sliding-4ths move inspired by rock pioneer Chuck Berry. To play it, simply barre your 1st finger across the top two strings while picking a stream of steady eighth-note triplets. Slide up to 8th (10th) position in bar 4 and catch the last note, the 12th-fret E (14th-fret F♯), with your 4th finger.

Heard throughout much of "Revolution" is a sort of shuffle pattern. To play the pattern that is used for the B (A) chord, barre your 1st finger at the 2nd (4th fret) on strings 3 and 4, periodically hammering on the 4th-fret F♯ (6th-fret G♯) with your 3rd finger. To play the same pattern for the F♯ (E) chord, simply shift the whole shape down a string set. And remember: The music has to swing!

Throughout the patterns, the meter is sometimes disrupted, shifting between 4/4 and 2/4. Be sure to scan ahead for these time changes, and when moving between them, try not to lose your sense of timing.

# Rock and Roll Hoochie Koo (page 183)

Singer-songwriter-guitarist Rick Derringer (who has been rocking for five decades) has lots of stamina. He was only a teenager when in 1965 his bubblegum group the McCoys scored a hit with "Hang On Sloopy." Not long after that, Derringer began working with guitarist Johnny Winter, who included Derringer's song "Rock and Roll Hoochie Koo" on the 1970 album *Johnny Winter And.* For his own 1973 album, *All American Boy,* Derringer redid the tune; this version, which became Derringer's signature song, is the source of the arrangement here.

"Rock and Roll Hoochie Koo" makes great use of *octaves* — pairs of the same notes in different frequencies. Octaves are first seen here in bars 5 and 6. One fingering can be used to play everything: Fret the higher note with your 3rd finger and the lower note with your 1st, arching that finger such that it mutes the in-between string. Incidentally, this same shape can be used to play octaves on strings 6 and 4. After you've learned how to play the music here, you might try adding some octaves in your own music — a great way to beef up single-note lines in any style.

The verse has some killer riffing in which bluesy double stops on strings 3–4 are pitted against a descending single-note lick from the A blues scale (A–C–D–E♭–E–G), identical to the A pentatonic minor scale (A–C–D–E–G) but including the flatted 5th (E♭). Everything is in 5th position, save for the 2nd-fret double stop, which you should grab with your 1st finger. Key to making this part sound rockin' is nailing the rhythms, so count carefully. The notes in the verse's first bar, for instance will fall on beat 1, the "and" of 1, 2, the "ee" of 2, the "uh" of 2, and so on. Also, be sure to include each fret-hand mute, for a bit of a funky feel.

In his solo Derringer goes for the jugular, kicking things off way up in the 17th position of the A minor pentatonic scale. The solo begins with a pair of *oblique* bends. To play them, depress the 20th-fret G with your 4th finger and the 19th-fret D with your 3rd finger, reinforced by your 1st and 2nd fingers. Pick both notes at once, keeping the G in place while bending the lower note up a whole step, to E. Learn the rest of the solo slowly, isolating any parts that give you rhythmic difficulty. Then, after you've learned the written solo, improvise some of your own lines in this section.

# Roxanne (page 208)

Loosely speaking, the Police were a punk band. But each member of the group was much more technically proficient than the typical punker. Guitarist Andy Summers was known for his cool, precise soundscapes on Police songs, influenced by a wide range of genres, everything from jazz to world music. From 1978's *Outlandos d'Amour,* "Roxanne" showcases Summers' tasty approach to rhythm guitar, his ability to play something interesting to support a melody without detracting from it.

In the intro and verses of "Roxanne," Summers plays a handful of voicings that are more jazzy than punk-sounding. Like the chord work in the Clash's "London Calling," most of these chords are gripped on the higher strings, staying out of range of the bass guitar. Strum the chords in downstrokes, and release fret-hand pressure after you play each chord, to cut its duration short as directed by the staccato markings. To play the Gsus4, the only chord you'll let ring, it might help to wrap your thumb around the neck to grab the 6th string's 3rd-fret G.

In contrast to the chords in the verse of "Roxanne," those of the chorus of "Roxanne" are more punk — mostly two-note power chords, containing just roots and 5ths — but are kind of elegant in their simplicity. This provides a nice harmonic and textural contrast to the other sections. The same grip can be used to play all these chords, 1st finger on the lower note and 3rd finger on the higher one. Although the chorus should be really easy to play, heads up on the syncopation that occurs in the bulk of the even measures, where you'll find a new chord on the "and" of beats 3 and 4.

# Runnin' with the Devil (page 222)

No book on classic rock guitar would be complete without a selection from Eddie Van Halen, the six-string wizard who, in the late 1970s, popularized the two-handed tapping technique. While "Runnin' with the Devil," from Van Halen's eponymous 1978 debut, doesn't have any tapping, it's got some of the killer rhythm work for which Van Halen is equally revered, to say nothing of a brief but blazing solo.

Eddie Van Halen most always tunes his guitar down a half step (low to high: Eb–Ab–Db–Gb–Bb–Eb). This gives him an ultra heavy sound and allows his strings to be bent and lowered with the whammy bar more easily. However, you don't need to detune unless you're playing along with the original record. Even then, if you're feeling lazy, a lot of software programs can take an mp3 and play it a half step higher so that you can play along without changing your tuning.

"Runnin' with the Devil" is basically made from just a couple of two-bar riffs. The first one, heard in the intro and chorus, is introduced in bar 3 of the song. To play it, barre the 5th-fret C chord with your 1st finger, moving it up to the 7th fret for the D chord. Keeping your 1st finger at the 7th fret, hammer on the G chord's 8th-fret G and 9th-fret B with, respectively, your 2nd and 3rd fingers. Move the entire shape up two frets for the A–E progression, barring your 1st finger at the 9th fret.

Heard in the verse, the other riff pits double-stop 3rds on strings 3 and 4 against the single notes G and A on the 6th and 5th strings. The most basic version of this riff is heard in the first two measures of the verse. Tackle it before delving into the more complex variations, involving random harmonics, trills, and other techniques that you learned about in other performance notes in this book. Then, when you play the song in its entirety, improvise your own versions on both riffs, as did Eddie Van Halen in the studio.

In his four-bar solo, Van Halen plays in a chordal manner. In the A5 bar, the phrase is based on a 2nd-inversion A major triad with the 5th in the bass, (E–A–C#) on strings 4–3. Use a 1st-finger barre to play the triad, adding the 15th and 17th notes with your 2nd and 4th fingers, respectively. Slide everything down two frets for the G5 measure, which has similar material based on a 2nd-inversion G major triad (D–G–B).

# Suffragette City *(page 213)*

Since the 1960s, rock star David Bowie has been known to continuously reinvent his musical and sartorial styles. Bowie started off as a typical folk-rocker and by 1972, with the introduction of his concept album *The Rise and Fall of Ziggy Stardust and the Spiders from Mars,* Bowie had become a flamboyantly androgynous performer with a hard-edged, experimental sound. From that album, "Suffragette City" is — despite its creator's undeniable oddness — filled with some classic guitar moves.

The verse of "Suffragette City" is made from the shuffle pattern popularized by such early rockers as Chuck Berry. To play it, fret each 6th-string note with your 1st finger and the lower and higher notes on string 5 with your 3rd and 4th fingers, respectively. Use all downstrokes throughout. Also, at the end of certain measures, a cool rhythm guitar trick is revealed: Picking an open string (or strumming the open strings) can buy you time to move to the next chord without disrupting the rhythm as you struggle to coordinate your fret and pick hands.

The solo is fairly straightforward, drawn mostly from the F♯ minor pentatonic scale (F♯–A–B–C♯–E) in 2nd position. But some of the bends might be a little tricky, so work through them slowly if necessary. For instance, in the first bar, prepare for the country-style bend by barring your 4th finger across strings 1 and 2 at the 5th fret. Then, use your 3rd finger, reinforced by your 1st and 2nd fingers, to play the 4th-fret bend. On the "and" of beat 1, for the *partial release* of the bend, release the string, not all the way to its standard position, but just enough that the note C is sounded. If you'd like, play the 3rd string's non-bent 5th-fret note for pitch reference.

One other thing to note in the solo: In the sixth measure, the indication *steady gliss.* calls for *glissando* — continuous sliding between notes. Here, move your 3rd finger along the 3rd string between the indicated notes, such that you can hear the discrete pitches between them.

# Time *(page 228)*

"Time," a song lamenting the increasingly swift passage of time as one ages, is from the psychedelic rock band Pink Floyd's *The Dark Side of the Moon.* That album is one of Floyd's most popular, as well as that of rock in general — in fact, it was on the U.S. charts for an amazing 762 consecutive weeks — that's 14 years!

The intro to "Time" features an awesomely economical approach to guitar playing. Instead of strumming chords or laying down riff upon riff, guitarist David Gilmour plays a simple single note line on strings 6 and 5, centered around held root notes and including the occasional ringing harmonic. This approach keeps the song's overall arrangement from becoming excessively cluttered. Remember the tired old maxim, that "less" is often "more."

Things get a little more involved in the verse, where basic chord shapes are decorated with some more complex ornaments and techniques. For example, in the fourth measure, the F♯m chord is negotiated with a quick lick from the F♯ minor pentatonic scale (F♯–A–B–C♯–E) in 2nd position. Later on in the 6th bar, the A chord is acknowledged with some sliding harmonic (simultaneous) 6ths from within the A major scale (A–B–C♯–D–E–F♯–G♯), some of which include the open G string. Fret the first pair (C♯–A) with your 2nd and 1st fingers on the 4th and 2nd strings, respectively, and all the rest with your 2nd and 3rd fingers. Because the rhythms are also more difficult here, you might need to subdivide — remember, count "One-ee-and-uh, two-ee-and-uh, three-ee-and-uh, four-ee-and-uh," and so on, paying close attention to which syllable each note should be assigned to.

The guitar solo is built largely from that basic rock scale — the first six measures are in the 2nd position of the F♯ pentatonic scale, with a brief excursion to a 5th-position box in bar 5; at bar 9 the solo travels up to the 14th position of the scale. But Gilmour's playing sounds anything but stock. For one, he has a highly personalized way of bending the strings and inflecting them with vibrato, so pay microscopically close attention to how those techniques sound on the original recording, and try to replicate them as closely as possible on your guitar.

Another reason the solo sounds a little nonstandard is that it features the occasional and skillful deployment of arpeggios. For more on arpeggios (broken chords), see "Highway Star". In bar 9, on beats 1 and 2, for example, an F♯m triad (F♯–A–C♯) is outlined; in the second half of bar 15, above the E chord, there are notes from a E major triad (E–G♯–B). Then, at the beginning of the interlude, there are some triads that acknowledge the chord changes: D major (D–F♯–A) for the D chord and the 7th and 5th (G♯ and E) of the Amaj7 chord.

# Up Around the Bend (page 239)

The rock band Creedence Clearwater Revival (CCR) emerged in the 1960s San Francisco Bay Area — a time and place rife with musical experimentation. But with their rootsy sound, influenced by country and Western, rockabilly, and swamp rock, CCR stood apart from the crowd. One of the group's most popular songs is 1970's "Up Around the Bend," from *Cosmo's Factory,* in which bandleader John Fogerty suggests that the listener come join him on the road.

Although the intro to "Up Around the Bend" has lots of notes, it's probably easier to play than it looks. All the music is based on arpeggios of the same basic chord grip, fingered, lowest note to highest, 2–1–1 on strings 3 through 1. Play this shape at the 10th fret in bars 1, 3, and 4, and at the 5th fret in the third measure. Keep the shape held for the duration of each chord, picking the individual notes as indicated, letting everything, including the open low notes, ring for as long as possible.

In the verse is a nice, subtle detail — each chord is decorated with its 6th (B on the D chord; F♯ on the A chord) on beats 2 and 4. In both cases, keep the basic chord shape held in place while adding the 6th with your 3rd finger, taking the time to pause and reflect on the different sonic qualities of the basic major chords and their 6th counterparts. Also, throughout try *pendulum strumming* — move your pick hand in a continuously alternating up-and-down eighth-note pattern, skipping over the strings on each beat 3, to prevent them from sounding.

Bars 1 and 3 of the brief guitar solo can be analyzed as centering around the notes of a G6 chord (G–B–D–E). Play this part with your 2nd, 1st, and 3rd fingers on, respectively, the 4th-, 3rd-, and 5th-fret notes. Meanwhile, the other measures come from the A major pentatonic scale (A–B–C♯–E–F♯), which you might recognize as simply being a reordering of the notes in the F♯ minor pentatonic scale (F♯–A–B–C♯–E). Look out for the pedal-steel inspired bends, which may take a bit of practice for you to be able to sound in tune.

# War Pigs (Interpolating Luke's Wall) (page 248)

With its down-tuned guitars, wailing solos, and macabre lyrics, Black Sabbath is the godfather of heavy metal. From 1970's *Paranoid,* "War Pigs (Interpolating Luke's Wall)" is a song about the dark side of mankind, its murderous and destructive nature. The tune is filled with powerful riffing and wailing soloing from Tony Iommi, the only consistent member of the band.

The pre-intro to "War Pigs" is in 12/8 meter — that's 12 eighth notes per measure, which can be counted "*One,* two, three; *two,* two, three; *three,* two, three; *four,* two, three," and so on. As for pitch content, the music switches back and forth between the basic harmonies of E and D. For the E chord at the end of both the first and second systems, depress the 7th-fret E and 6th-fret G♯ with, respectively, either your 2nd and 1st fingers or 3rd and 2nd, hammering on the 7th-fret A with either your 3rd or 4th finger. Note that the A is the E chord's 4th and that this move hints briefly at an Esus4 chord (E–A–B).

Played faster, the intro and verse are in 4/4 and feature a sort of *stop time* — a disruption of the expected rhythmic pattern. The guitar makes a statement on the downbeat of each odd measure, while the vocals fill in the gaps. As you did in "Bad Case of Loving You," refrain from noodling during these extended rests and turn your attention to the vocalist's part.

Although it is played in open position, the bridge is a bit more complicated. Take things really slowly in learning it, subdividing if you need — remember, for instance, in the first bar, open Es will fall on the "ee" and the "uh" of beat 3. Play the 2nd-fret notes with whatever fret-hand fingering is most comfortable to you, and be sure to observe the palm-muting throughout on string 6, to keep the riff nice and crisp.

The guitar solo begins with a cool strategy — notes from the E Mixolydian mode (E–F♯–G♯–A–B–C♯–D) are played atop a low open E. That mode is similar to the E major scale (E–F♯–G♯–A–B–C♯–D♯), but contains a flatted 7th (D). That one adjustment found in the mode makes for a more mysterious sound in this context. To hear what we're talking about, whenever you see the note D natural in the transcription, try playing a D♯ instead.

# White Room (page 242)

Guitarist Eric Clapton was considered by many to be the top guitarist of the mid-1960s, and his fierce rock-blues playing even inspired the graffito text and subsequent saying "Clapton is God." Listening to "White Room" (*Wheels of Fire,* 1968), recorded with Clapton's power trio Cream, can help you to understand the comparison.

In its intro and interlude, "White Room" features a time signature that is uncommonly heard in mainstream rock: 5/4, which consists of five quarter notes per measure. Because the rhythms in these sections are plain, the meter should be simple to count — tap five beats in each bar, and make sure to subtract a beat in the 4/4 bar that precedes the verse. Or, if you're playing along with the original recording, you should have an easy enough time by just following drummer Ginger Baker's tom-tom hits.

The verse of "White Room" contains another of those two-bar riffs played with a number of small, improvised variations. So in successfully tackling the first two measures of the verse, you'll have essentially learned the entire section. One tip: Although the notes of the Csus2 chord aren't played at once, keep the chord grip held for the entire duration of the chord.

"White Room" has one of the greatest wah-wah solos ever recorded, based on the D minor pentatonic scale (D–F–G–A–C), primarily in 10th position. In case you're unfamiliar with a wah-wah pedal, it's a foot-operated device that alters the tone of your guitar's signal. The heel-down position of the pedal makes for a bass-heavy sound, whereas the toe-down position sounds more trebly. Moving the pedal back and forth makes your guitar's sound sweep across the frequency spectrum, creating the voicelike wah-wah sound for which the pedal is named.

If using a wah-wah pedal is new to you, first learn the solo without it. Then incorporate the pedal in graduating degrees of complexity: Begin by rocking it back and forth in quarter notes as you play through the section, then move on to an eighth-note-based motion. After you get the hang of it, try adding some more sophisticated wah-wah work to the solo based on the phrasing of the guitar lines.

# Jungle Love

Words and Music by Lonnie Turner and Greg Douglas

Open A tuning:
(low to high) E-A-E-A-C#-E

**Intro**
**Moderately fast** ♩ = 144

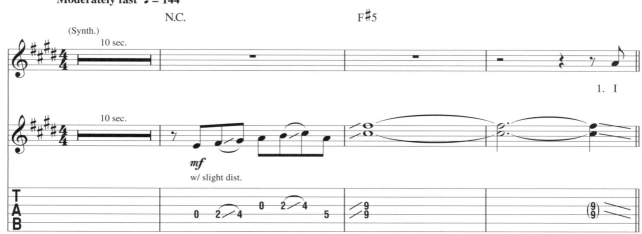

**§ Verse**

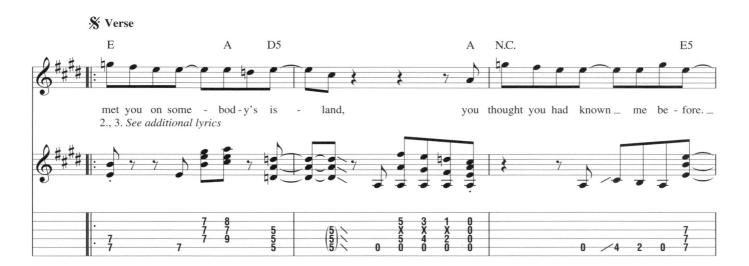

met you on some - bod-y's is - land,  you thought you had known \_ me be - fore. \_
2., 3. *See additional lyrics*

\_\_\_ I brought you a crate \_ of pa - pa - ya  that

*3rd time, omit slides & slurs.

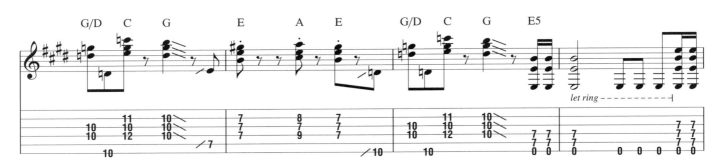

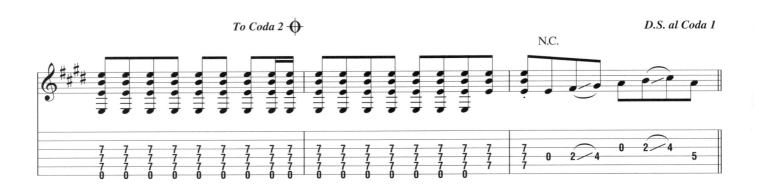

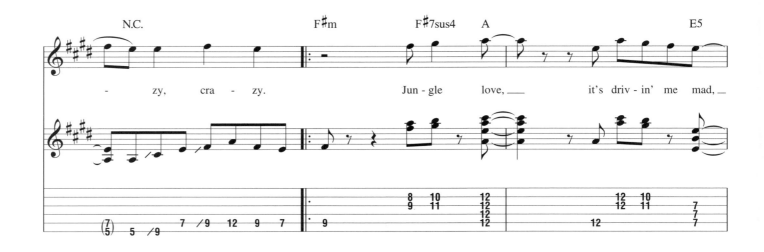

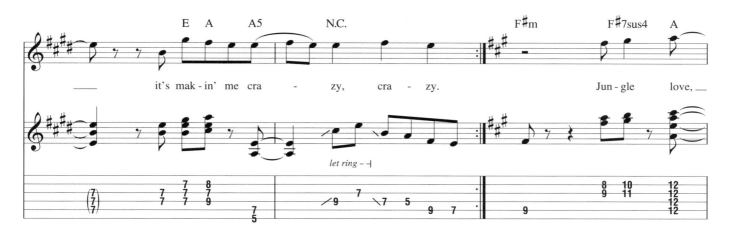

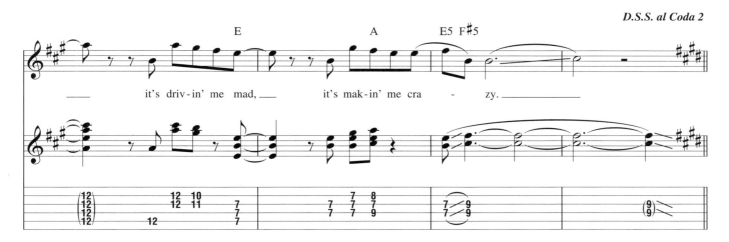

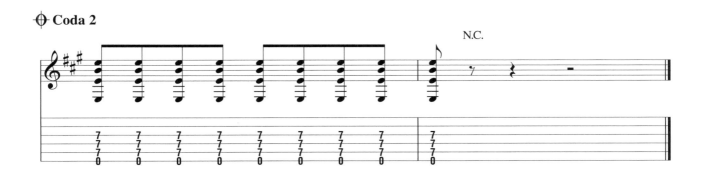

*Additional Lyrics*

2. But lately you live in the jungle,
   I never see you alone.
   But we need some definite answers,
   So I thought I would write you a poem.
   The question to ev'ryone's answer
   Is usually asked from within.
   But patterns of the rain, and the truth they contain
   That I've written my life on your skin.

3. You treat me like I was your ocean,
   You swim in my blood when it's warm.
   My cycles of circular motion
   Protect you and keep you from harm.
   You live in a world of illusion
   Where ev'rything's peaches and cream.
   We all face the scarlet conclusion,
   But we spend our time in a dream.

# La Grange

Words and Music by Billy F Gibbons, Dusty Hill and Frank Lee Beard

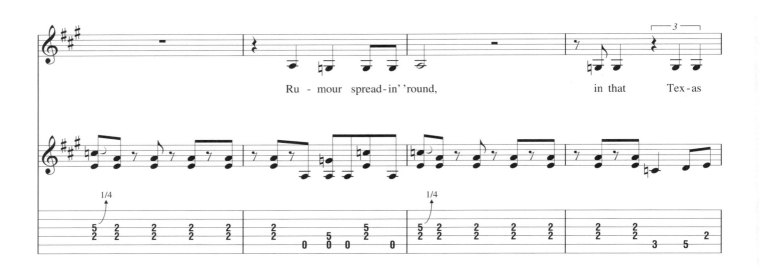

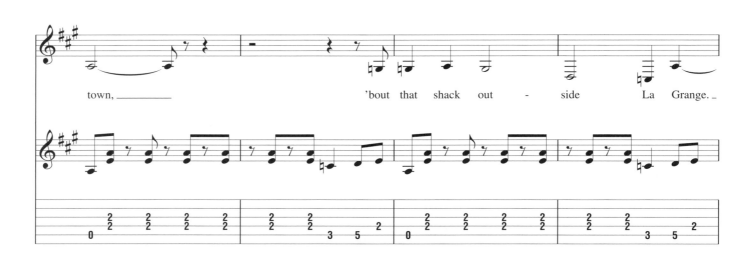

Spoken: And you know what I'm talk-in' a-bout.    Just    let   me know

if   you __ wan - na   go __                                    to   that

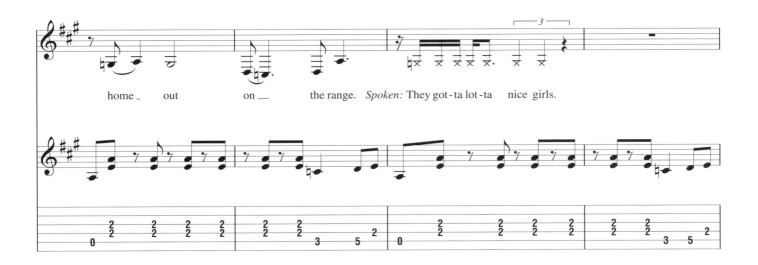

home _ out      on __    the range. *Spoken:* They got-ta lot-ta   nice girls.

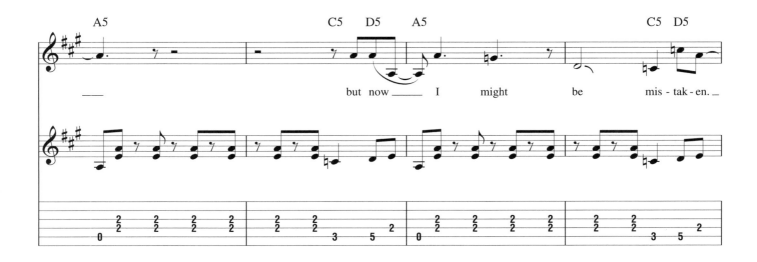

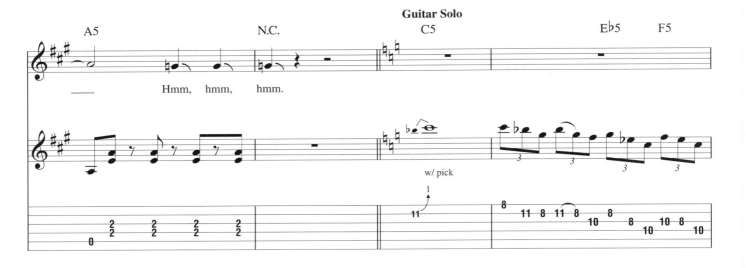

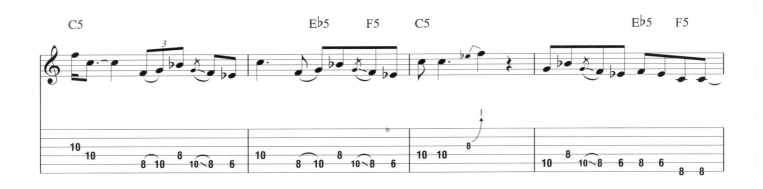

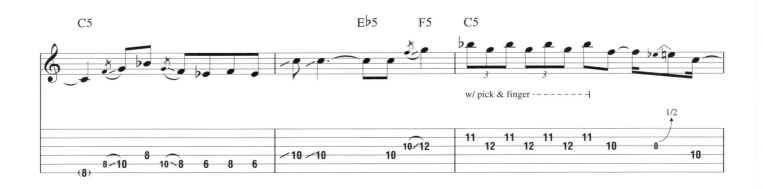

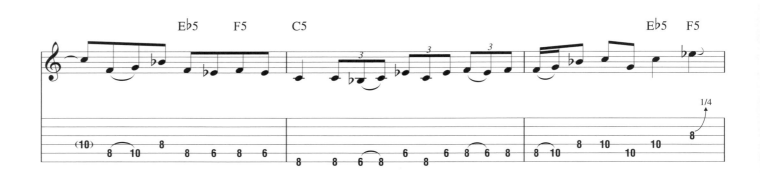

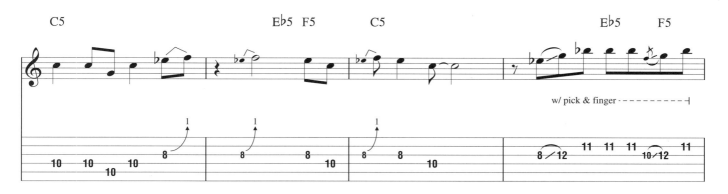

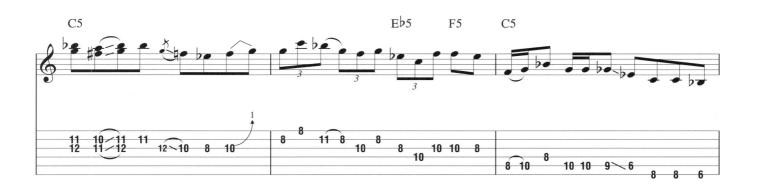

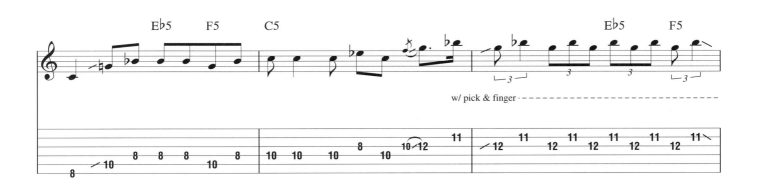

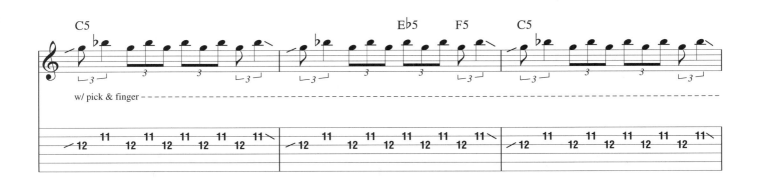

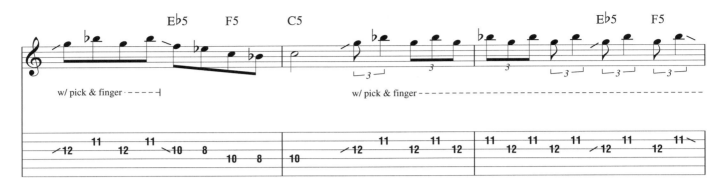

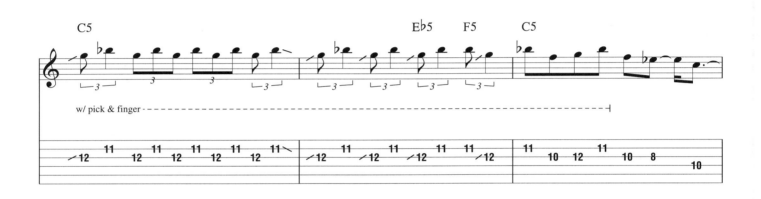

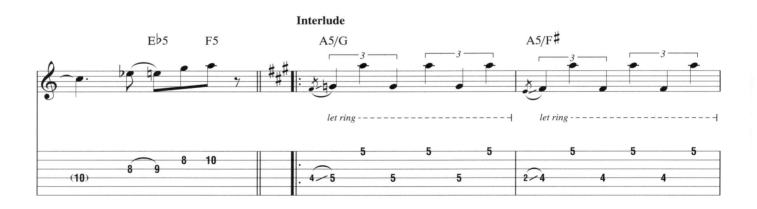

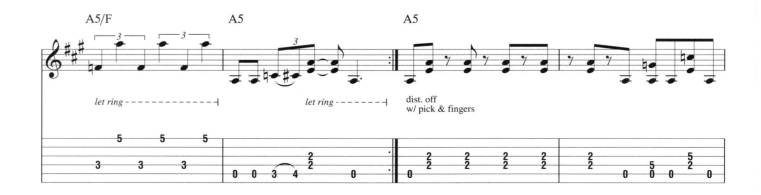

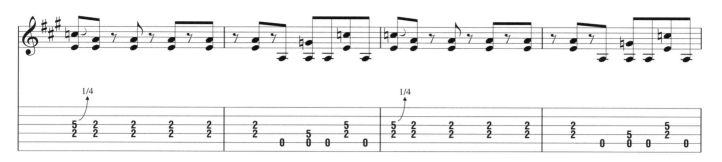

**Outro-Guitar Solo**

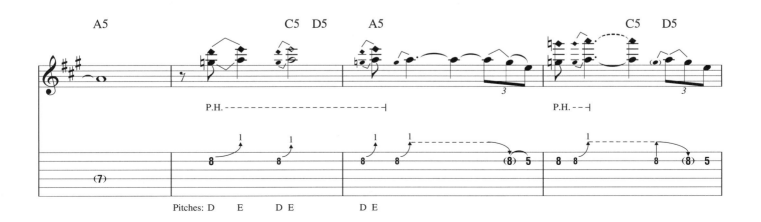

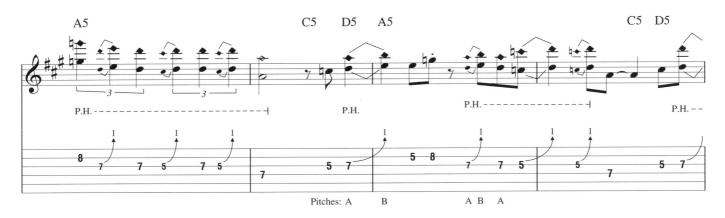

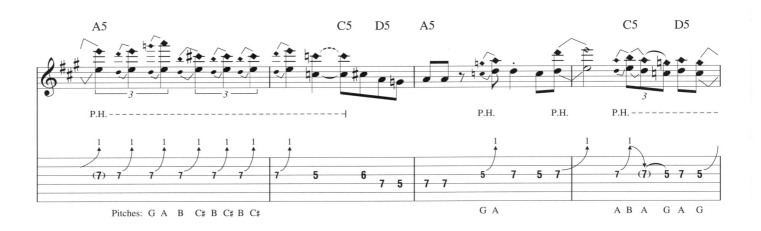

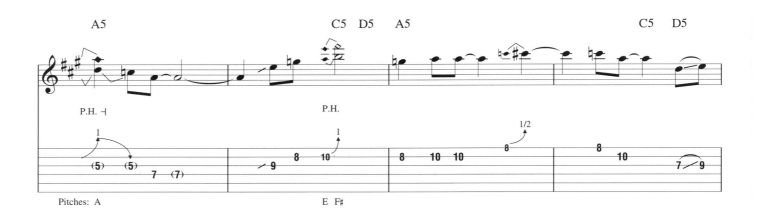

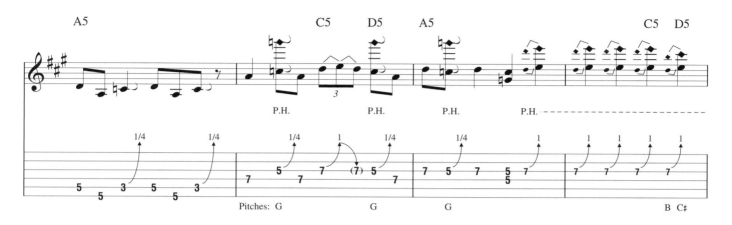

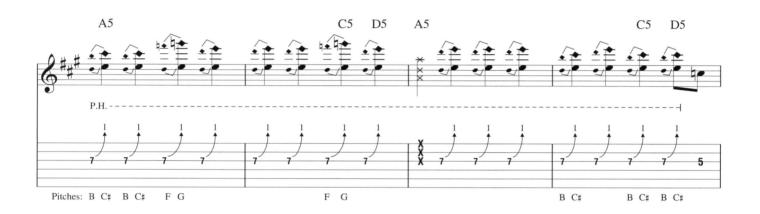

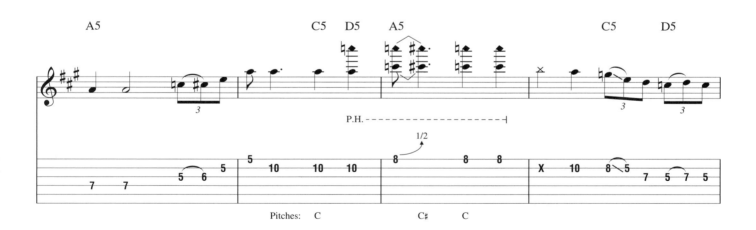

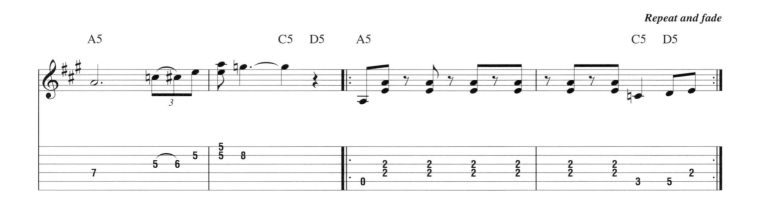

# Lay Down Sally

Words and Music by Eric Clapton, Marcy Levy and George Terry

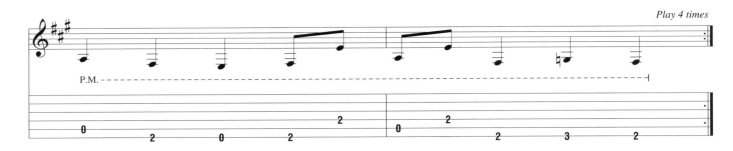

1. There is noth - ing that _____ is wrong _____ in
2., 3. *See additional lyrics*

want - ing you _____ to stay _____ here _____ with

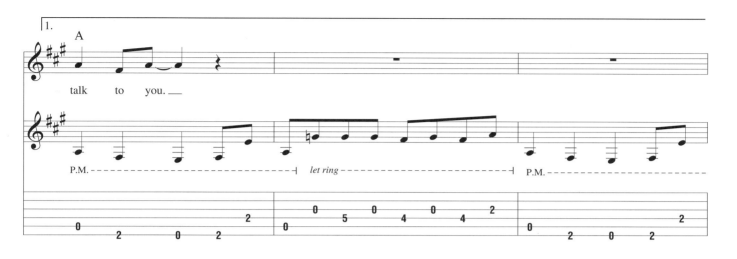

talk    to    you. ___

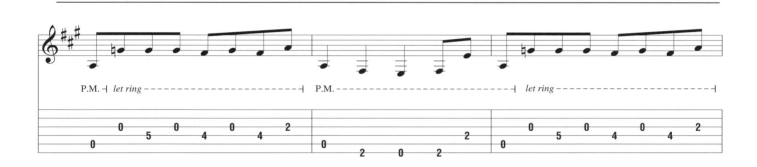

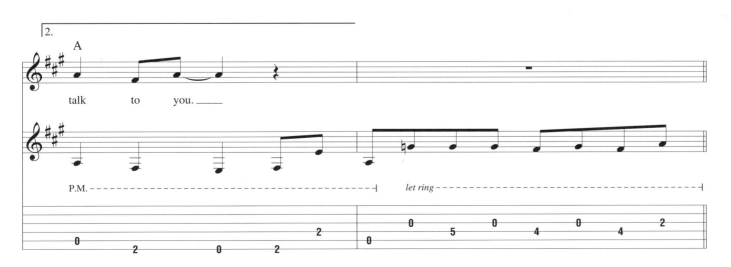

talk    to    you. ___

**Guitar Solo**

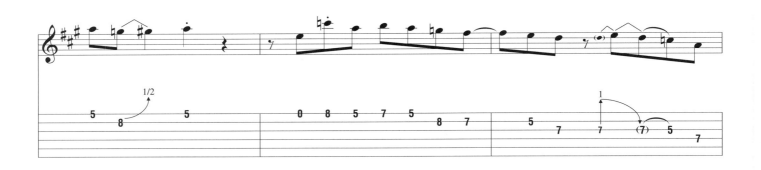

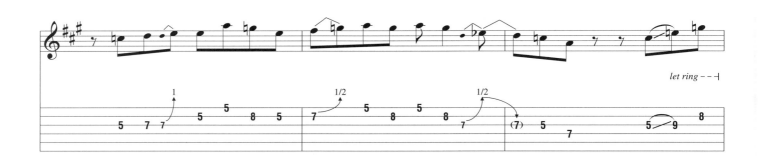

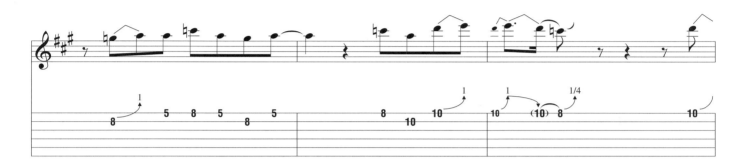

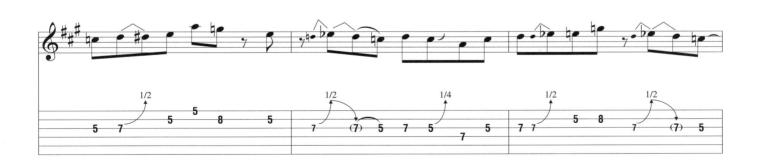

*Additional Lyrics*

2. Sun ain't nearly on the rise,
And we still got the moon and stars above.
Underneath the velvet skies,
Love is all that matters. Won't you stay with me?
And don't you ever leave.

3. I long to see the morning light
Coloring your face so dreamily.
So don't you go and say goodbye,
You can lay your worries down and stay with me.
And don't you ever leave.

# Oye Como Va

Words and Music by Tito Puente

**Intro**
**Moderate Latin** ♩ = 126

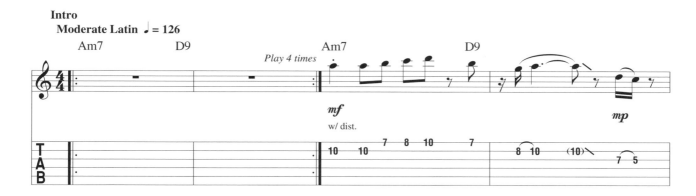

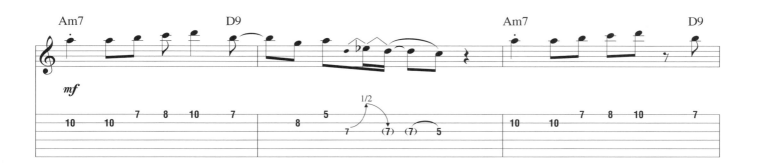

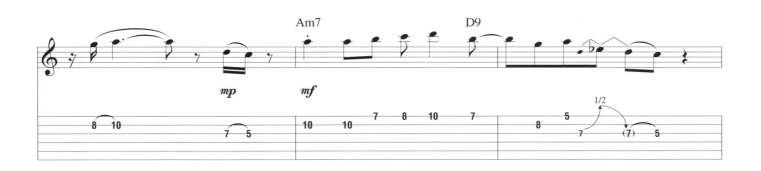

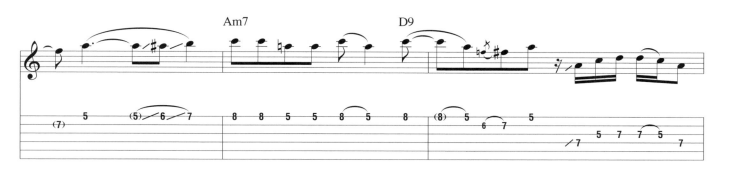

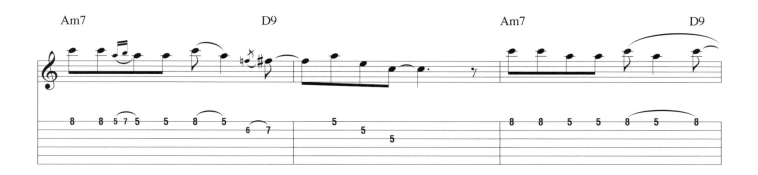

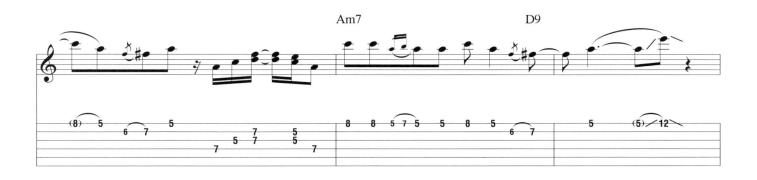

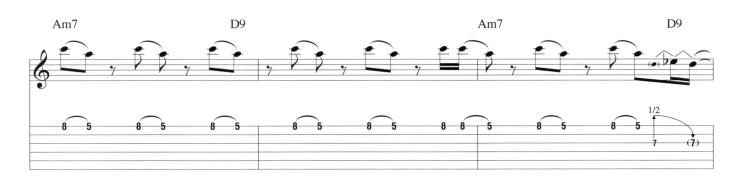

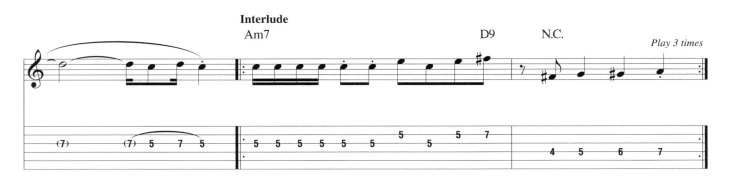

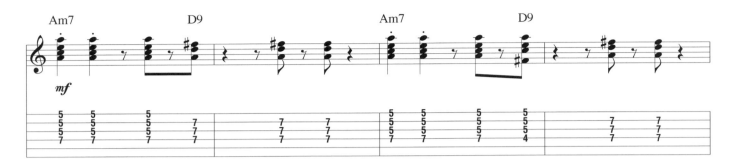

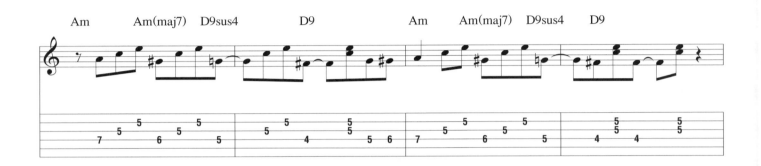

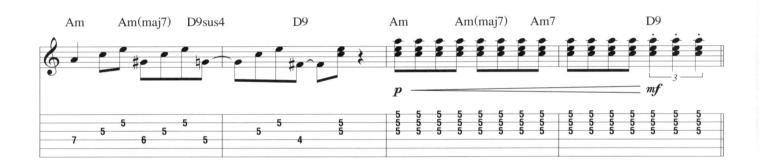

**Organ Solo**

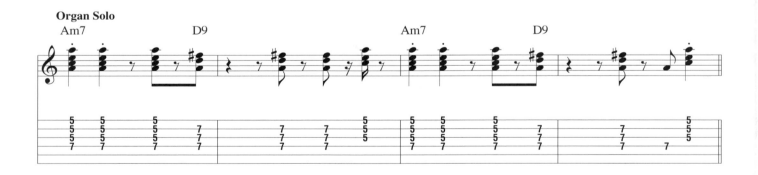

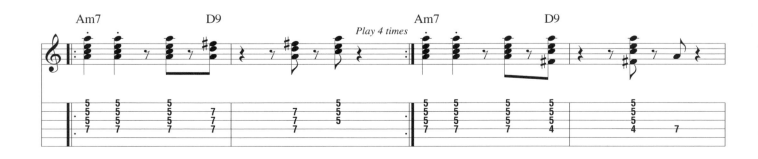

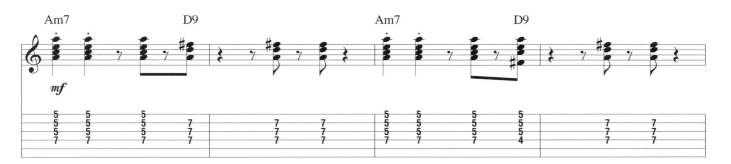

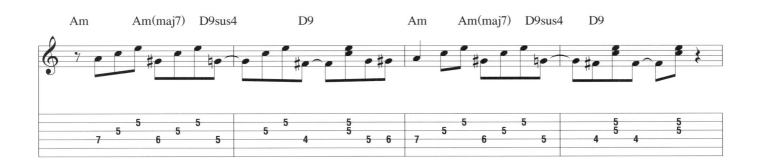

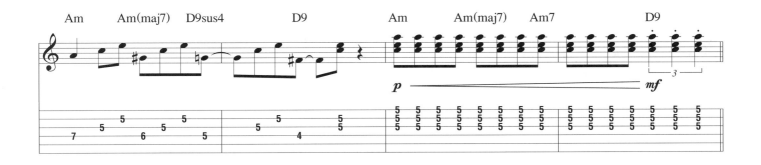

**Organ Solo**

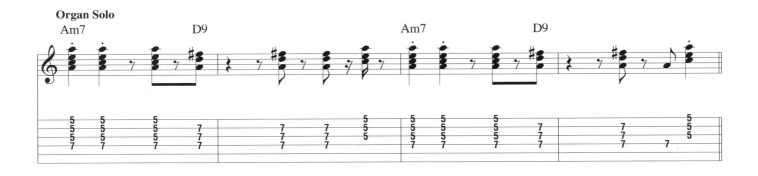

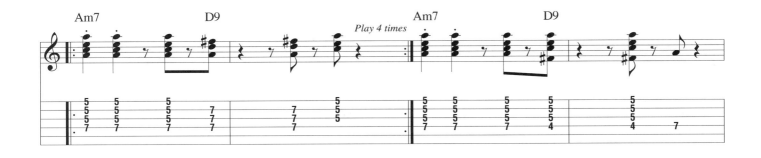

**Bridge**

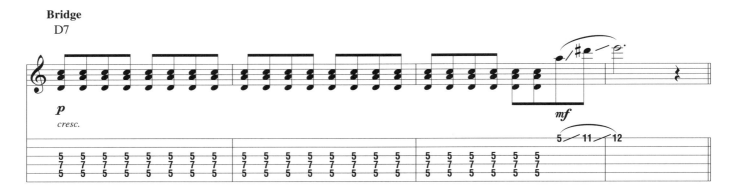

**Guitar Solo**

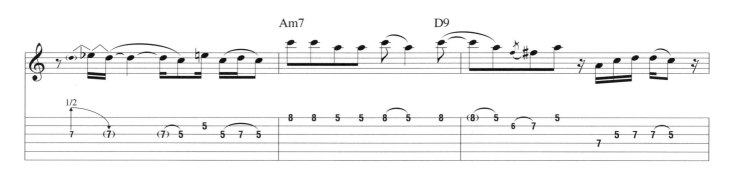

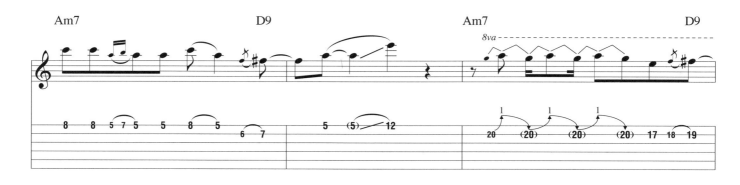

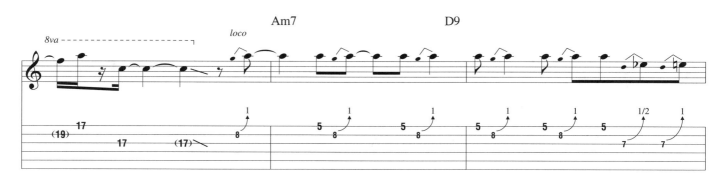

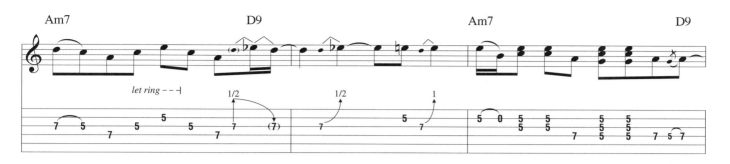

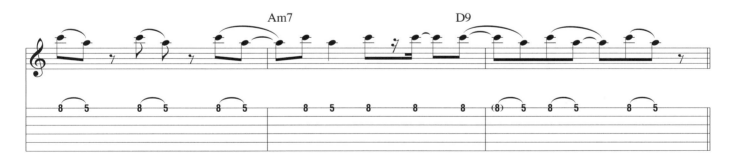

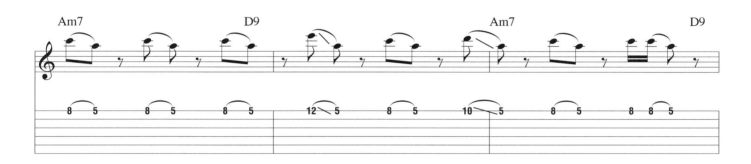

**Outro**

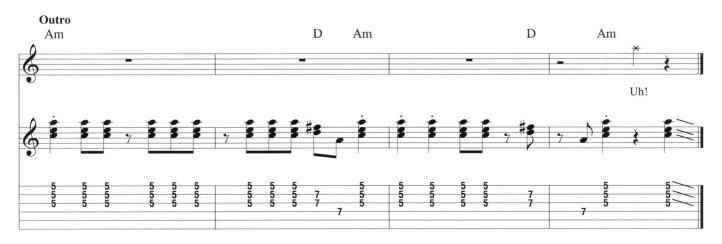

# London Calling

Words and Music by Joe Strummer, Mick Jones, Paul Simonon and Topper Headon

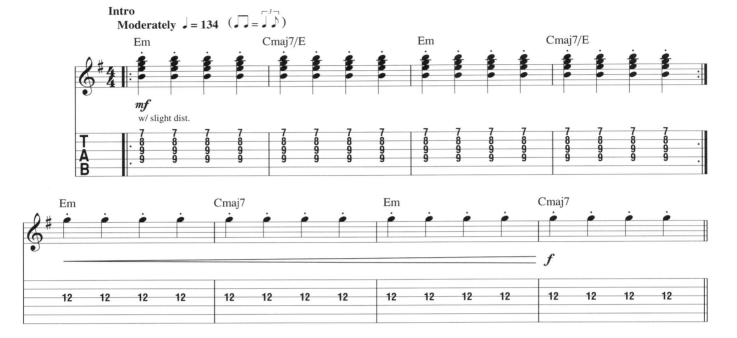

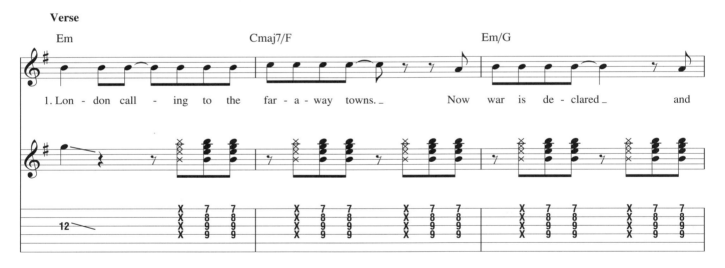

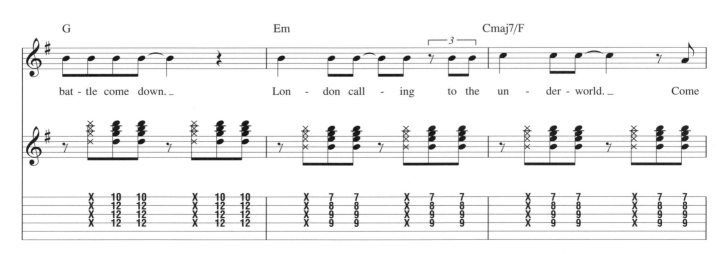

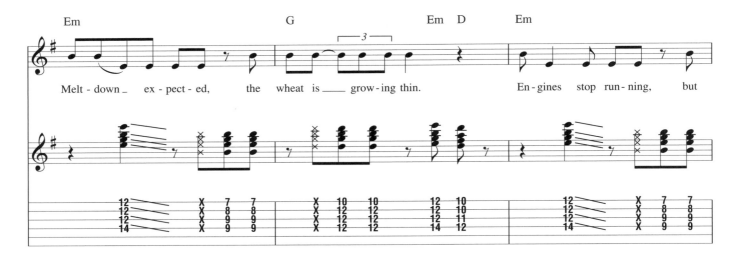

Melt - down _ ex - pect - ed,    the    wheat is _ grow - ing thin.    En - gines stop run - ning,    but

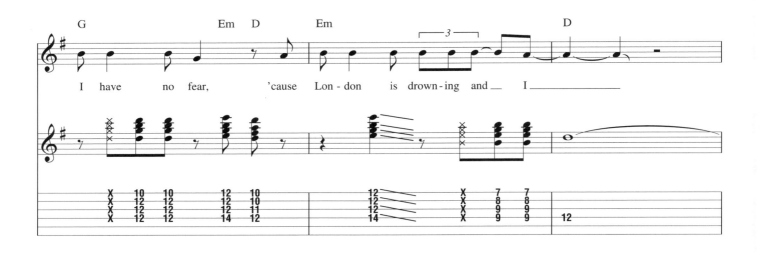

I    have    no    fear,    'cause Lon - don    is drown - ing and _ I _____

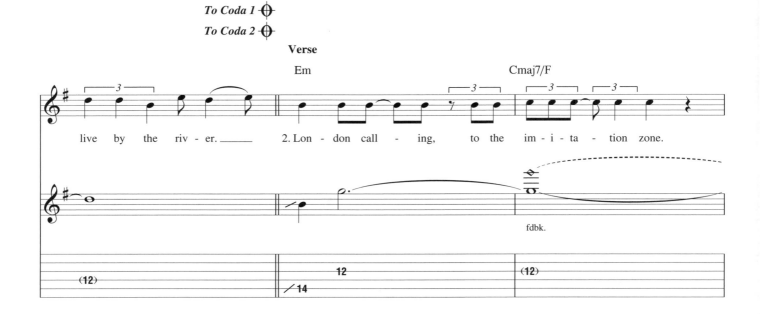

*To Coda 1*
*To Coda 2*
**Verse**

live    by    the    riv - er. _____ 2. Lon - don call - ing,    to the    im - i - ta - tion zone.

fdbk.

Em/G            G            Em

For - get it broth - er,    you can   go it a - lone. \_        Lon - don call - ing,   to the

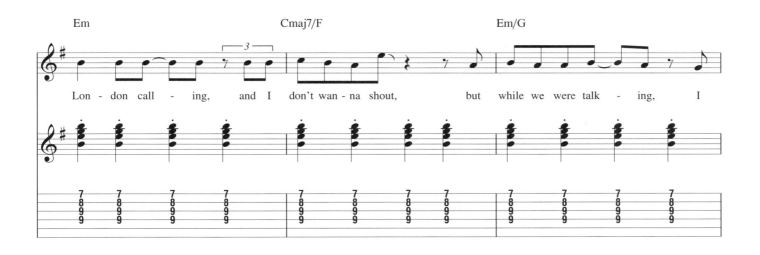

Gtr. tacet

Cmaj7/F         Em/G         G

zom - bies of death, \_    quit hold - ing out    and draw an - oth - er breath. \_

Em           Cmaj7/F        Em/G

Lon - don call - ing,   and I   don't wan - na shout,    but while we were talk - ing,   I

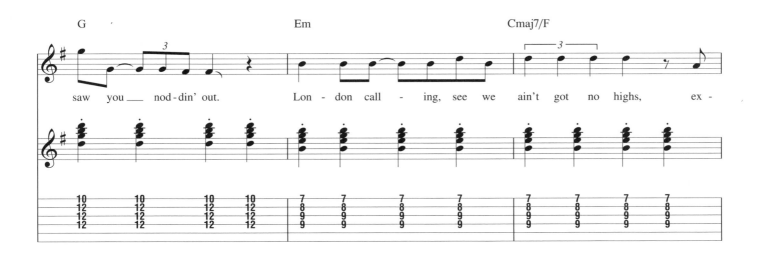

G            Em            Cmaj7/F

saw you \_ nod - din' out.    Lon - don call - ing, see we ain't got no highs,    ex -

*D.S. al Coda 1*

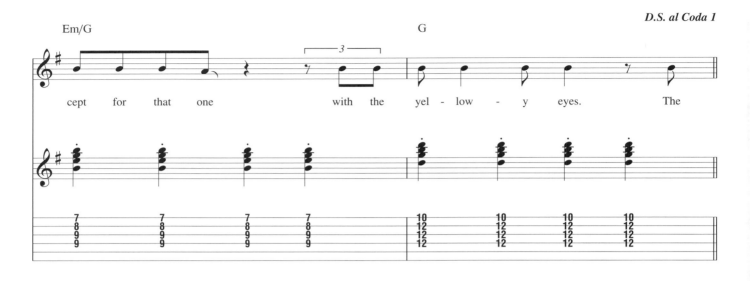

cept    for    that    one        with    the    yel - low - y    eyes.        The

**⊕ Coda 1**

**Interlude**

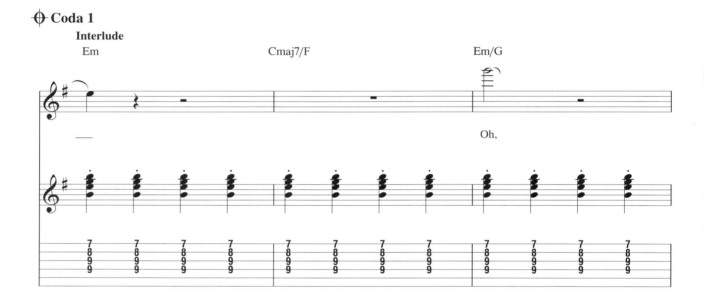

__        Oh,

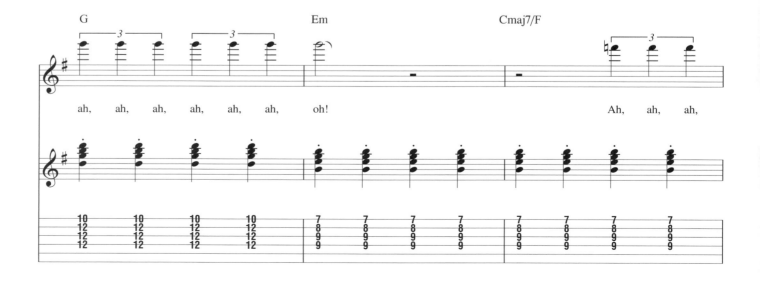

ah,    ah,    ah,    ah,    ah,    ah,    oh!                Ah,    ah,    ah,

**Guitar Solo**

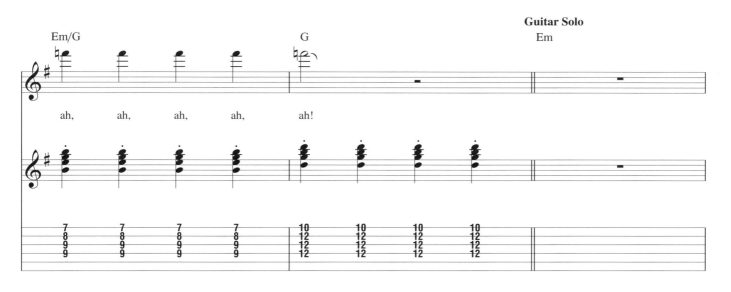

ah,   ah,   ah,   ah,   ah!

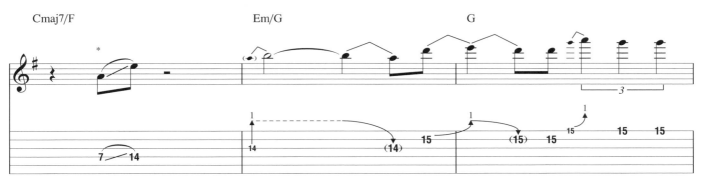

*Backwards guitar arranged for standard, next 7 meas.

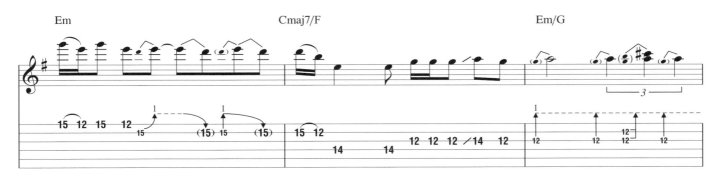

**Coda 2**

**D.S. al Coda 2**

**Interlude**

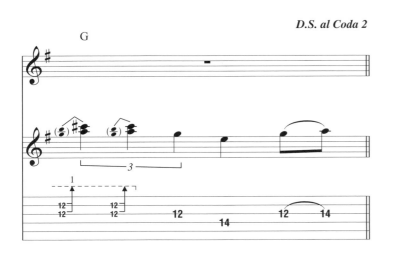

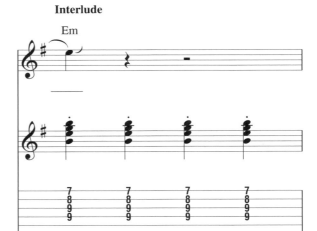

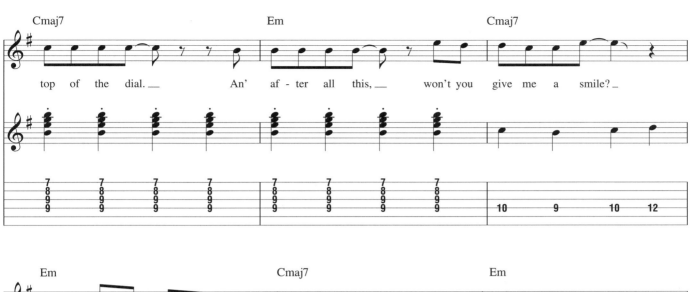

top of the dial. ___ An' af - ter all this, ___ won't you give me a smile? ___

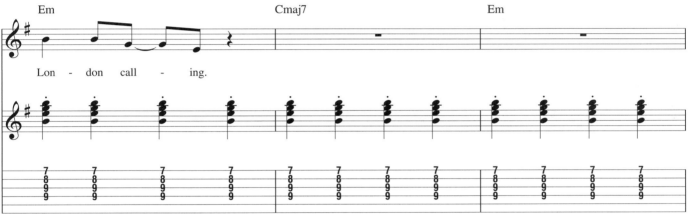

Lon - don call - ing.

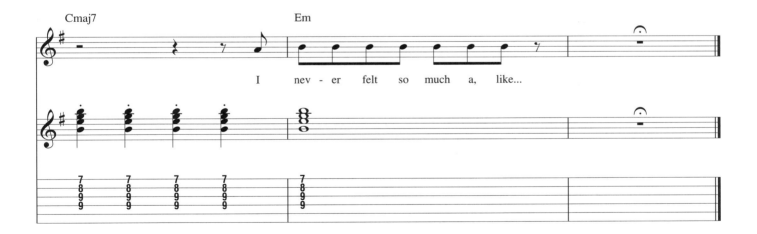

I nev - er felt so much a, like...

*Additional Lyrics*

*Chorus* 2., 3. The ice age is coming, the sun's zooming in.
Engines stop running, the wheat is growing thin.
A nuclear error, but I have no fear,
'Cause London is drowning and I, I live by the river.

# Peace of Mind

Words and Music by Tom Scholz

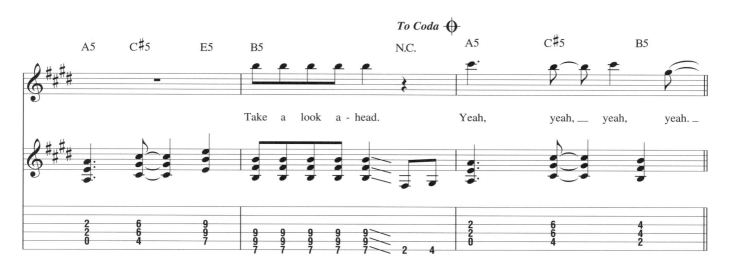

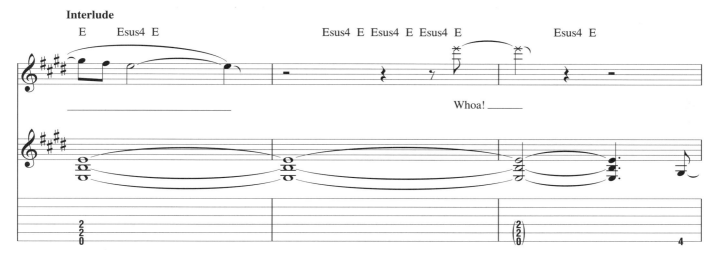

**Coda**

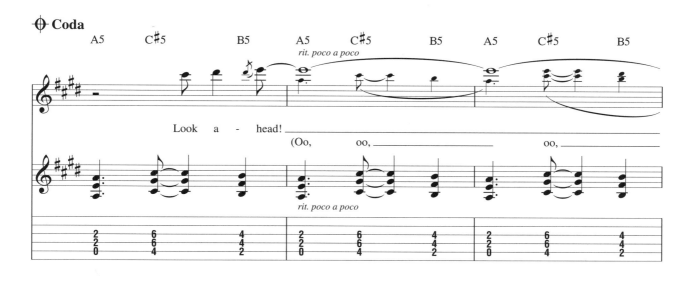

Look a - head! (Oo, oo, oo,

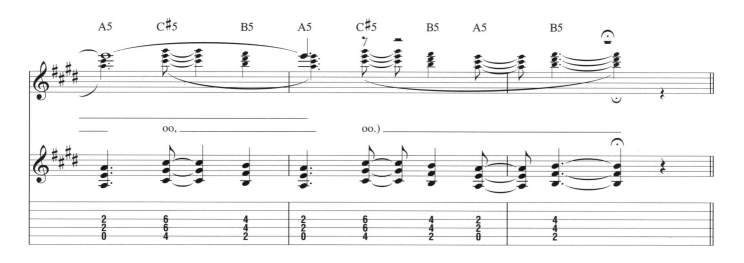

oo, oo.)

**Breakdown**
**A tempo**

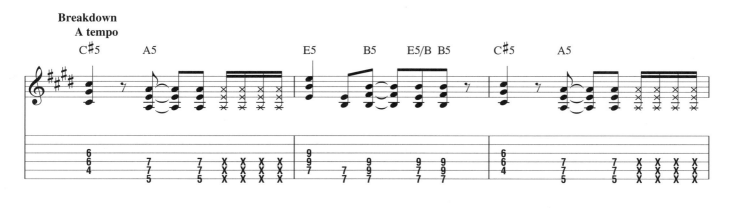

**Outro**

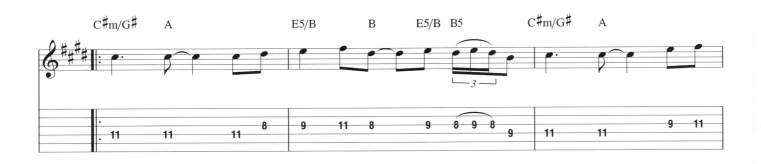

*Begin fade*

*Repeat and fade*

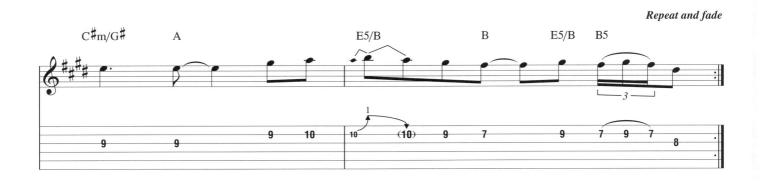

*Additional Lyrics*

3. Now ev'rybody's got advice they just keep on givin';
   Doesn't mean too much to me.
   Lots of people out to make-believe they're livin';
   Can't decide who they should be.

# Rock and Roll Hoochie Koo

Words and Music by Rick Derringer

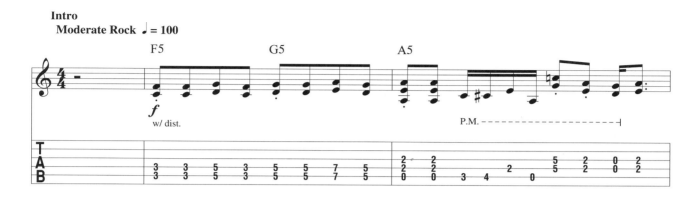

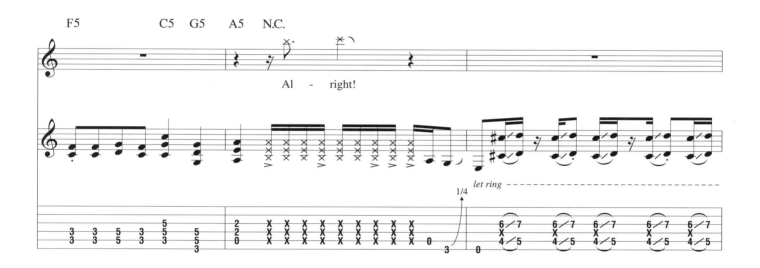

Al - right!

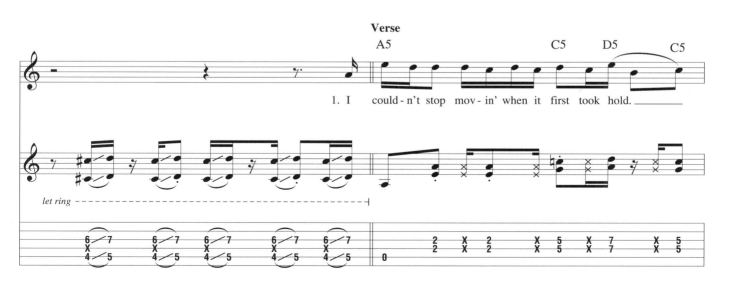

1. I could-n't stop mov-in' when it first took hold. ___

**Guitar Solo**

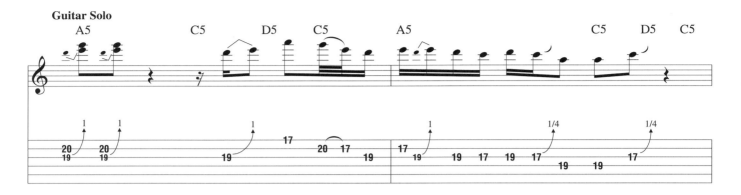

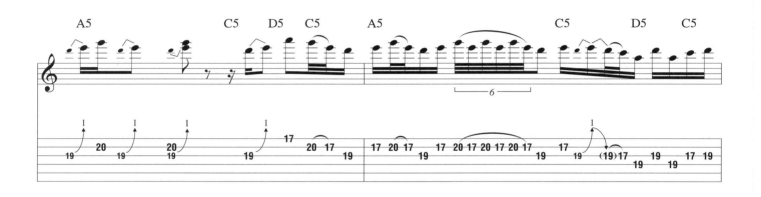

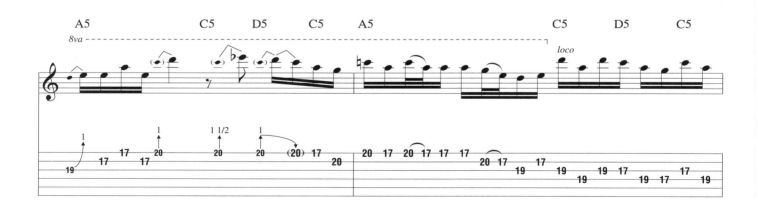

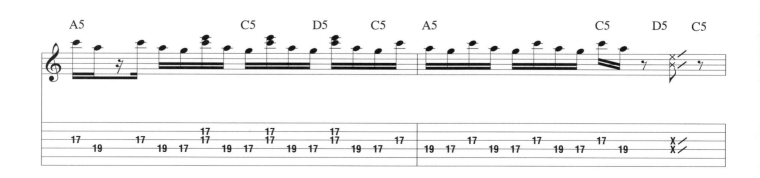

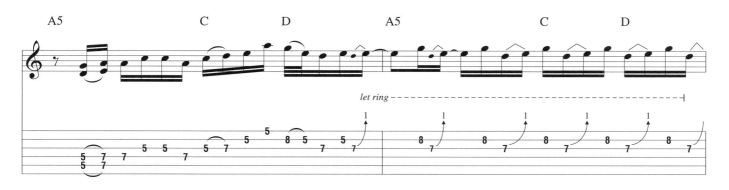

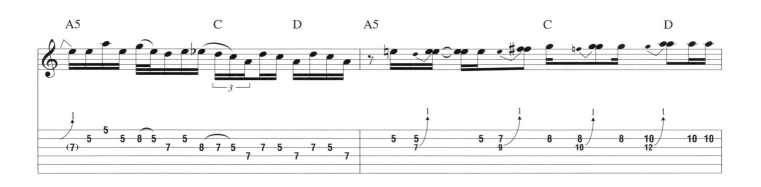

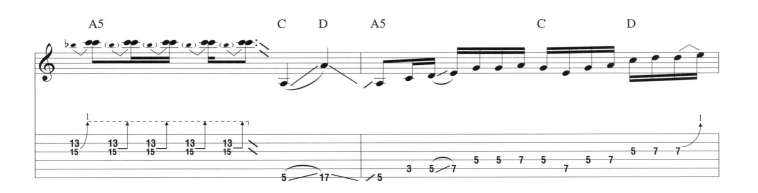

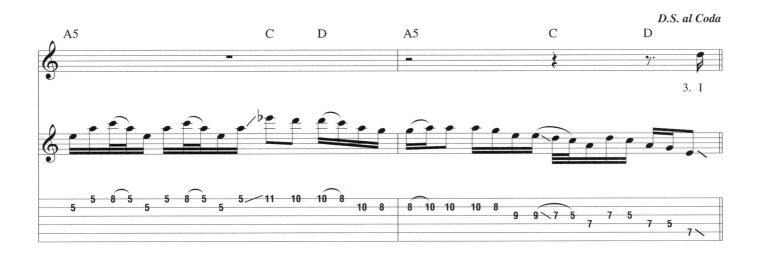

Coda

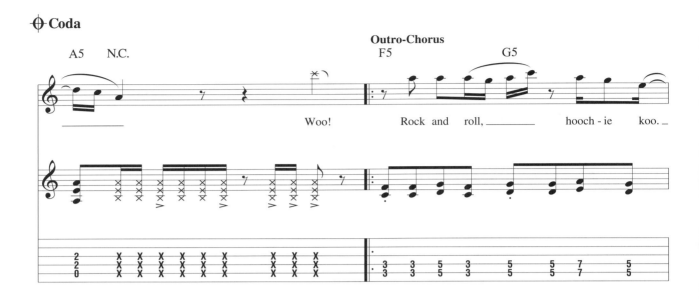

Woo! Rock and roll, _____ hooch - ie koo. _

Law - dy ma - ma, light my fuse. _____
Truck on out ____ and spread the news, _____          yeah,

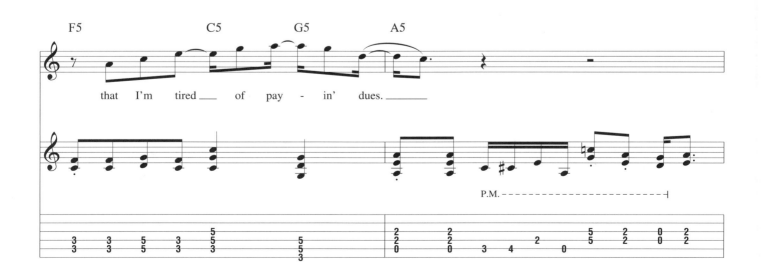

that I'm tired ___ of pay - in' dues. _____

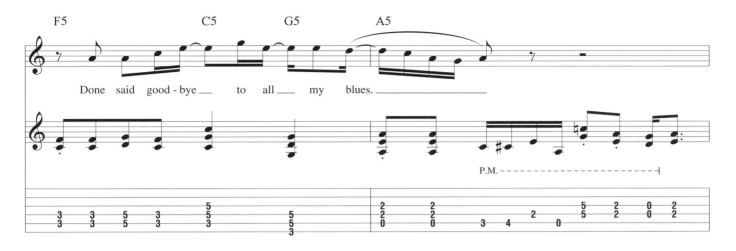

Done said good - bye ___ to all ___ my blues. ___

Law - dy ma - ma, light my fuse. ___ Woo! ___

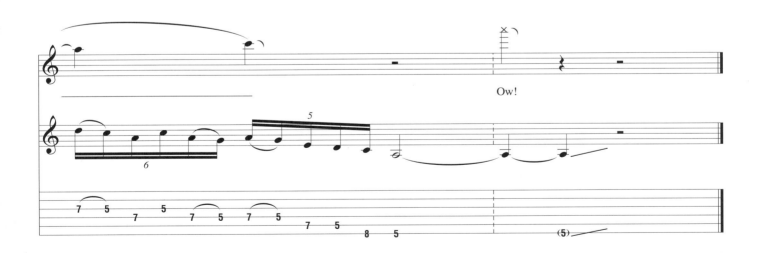

Ow!

*Additional Lyrics*

3. I hope you all know what I'm talkin' about.
   The way they wiggle that thing really knocks me out.
   Gettin' high all the time; hope you all are too.
   Come on little 'cuz, I'm gonna do it to you.

# Reeling in the Years

Words and Music by Walter Becker and Donald Fagen

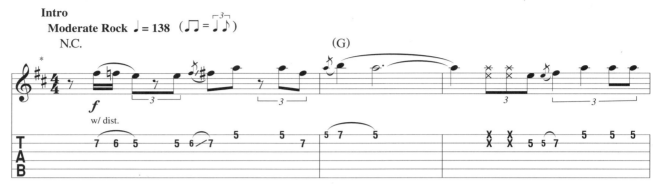

*Key signature denotes A Mixolydian.

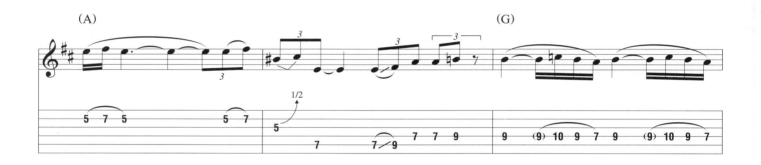

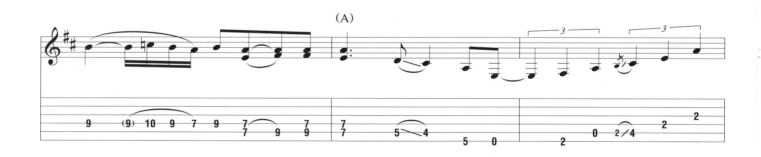

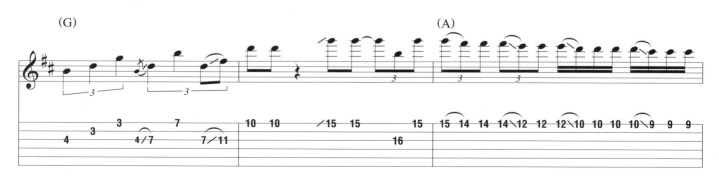

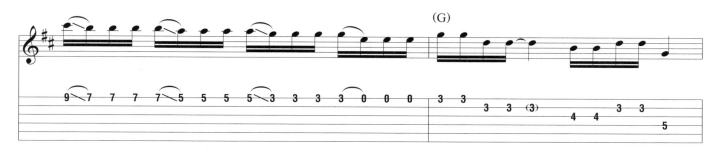

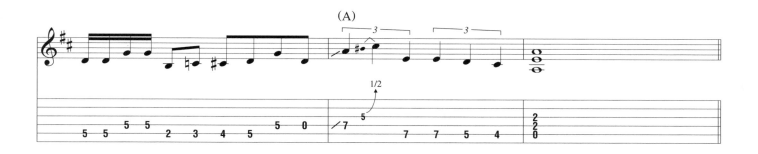

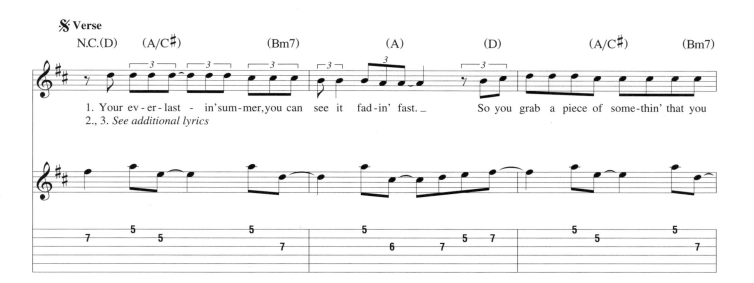

**Verse**

N.C.(D)    (A/C♯)        (Bm7)        (A)        (D)        (A/C♯)        (Bm7)

1. Your ev-er-last-in'sum-mer,you can see it fad-in' fast. _     So you grab a piece of some-thin' that you
2., 3. *See additional lyrics*

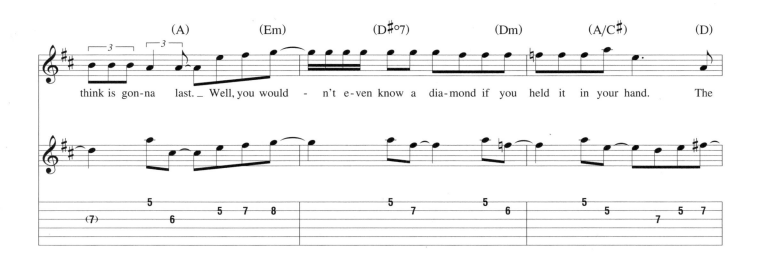

(A)        (Em)        (D♯°7)        (Dm)        (A/C♯)        (D)

think is gon-na last. _ Well, you would - n't e-ven know a dia-mond if you held it in your hand. The

stow-in' a-way the time? ___ Are you gath-er-in' up the tears? ___

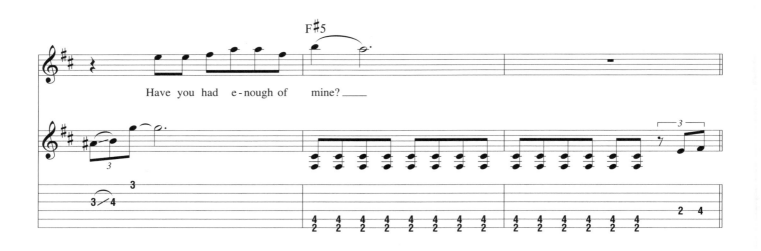

Have you had e-nough of mine? _____

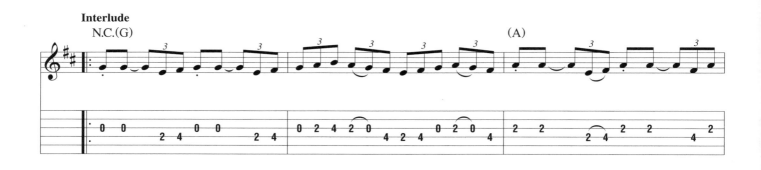

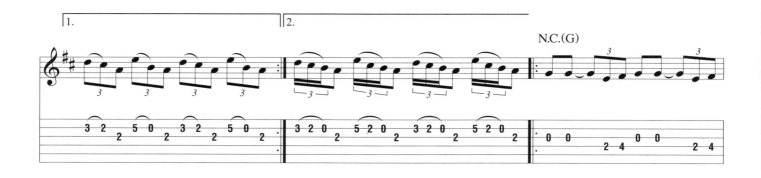

**Guitar Solo**

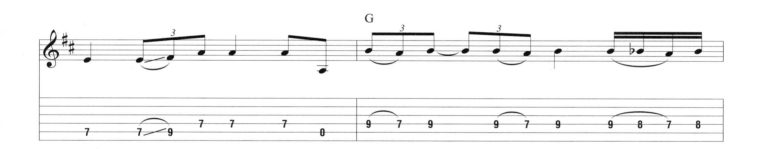

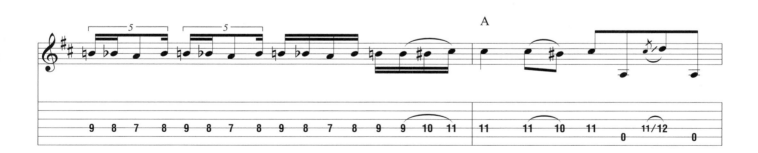

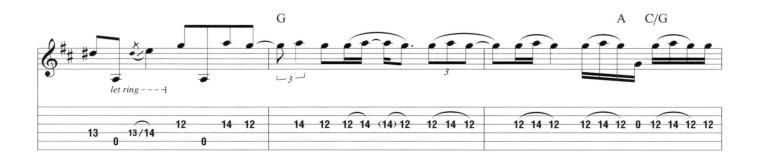

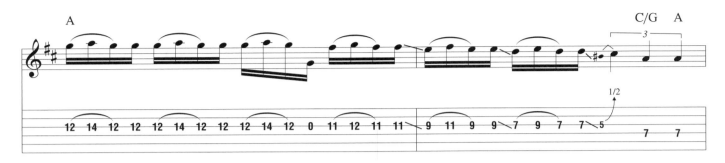

*D.S. al Coda 2*

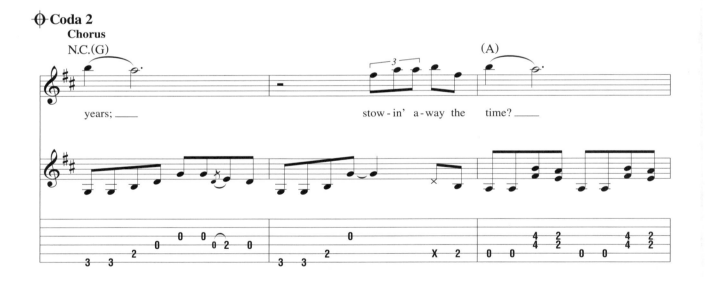

**Coda 2**

**Chorus**

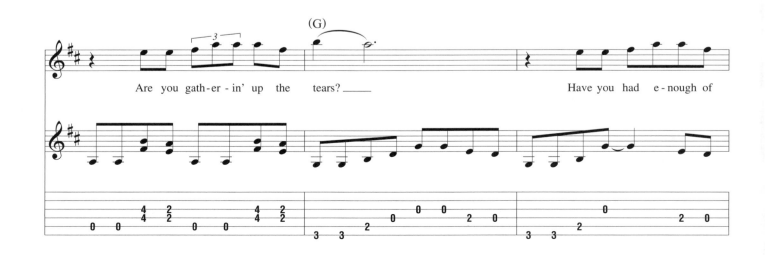

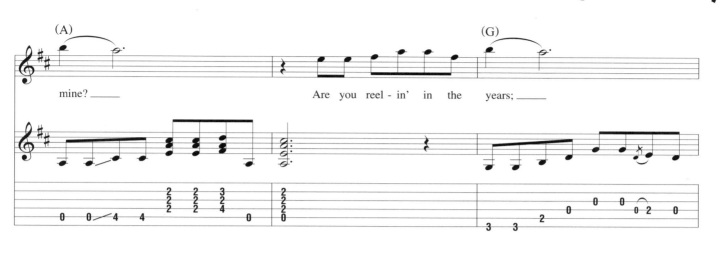

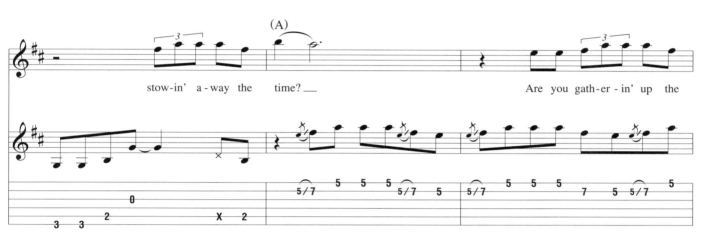

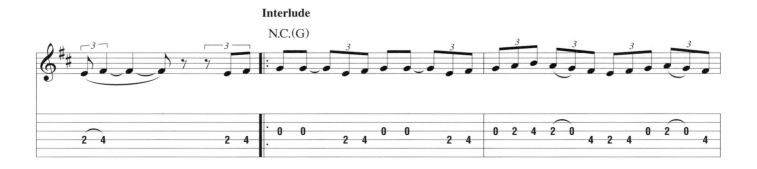

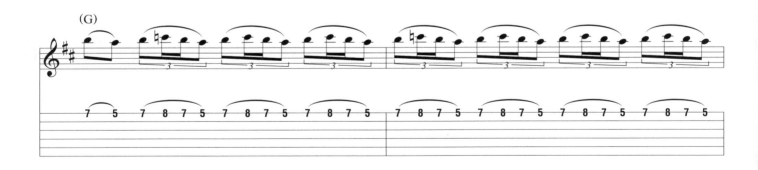

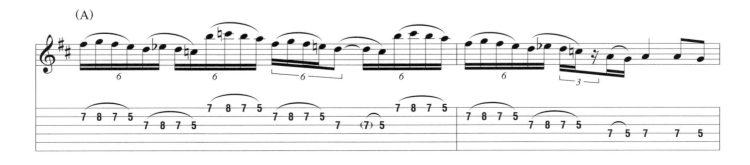

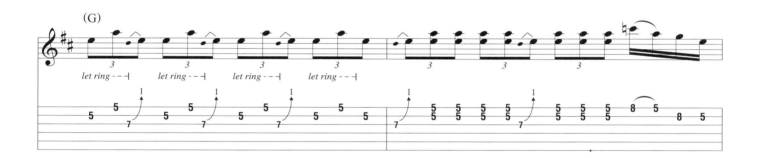

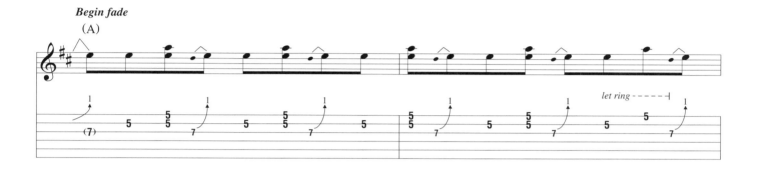

*Additional Lyrics*

2. You've been tellin' me you're a genius since you were seventeen.
   In all the time I've known you I still don't know what you mean.
   The weekend at the college didn't turn out like you planned.
   The things that pass for knowledge I can't understand.

3. I've spent a lot of money and I've spent a lot of time.
   The trip we made to Hollywood is etched upon my mind.
   After all the things we've done and seen you find another man.
   The things you think are useless I can't understand.

## *Revolution*

### Words and Music by John Lennon and Paul McCartney

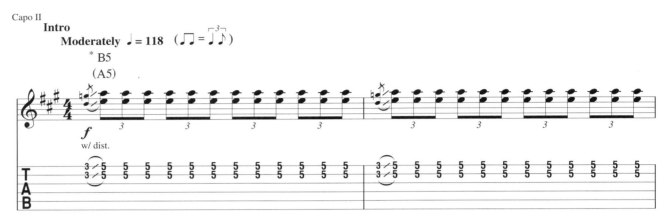

*Symbols in parentheses represent chord names respective to capoed guitar.
Symbols above reflect actual sounding chords. Capoed fret is "0" in tab.

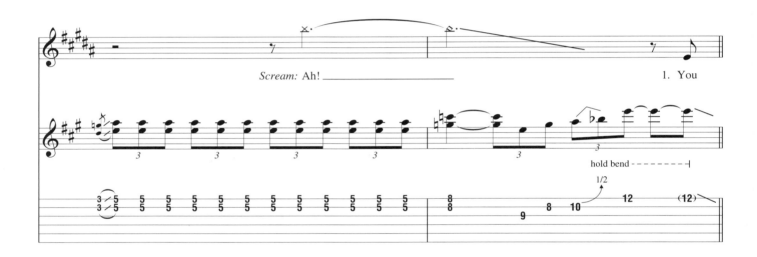

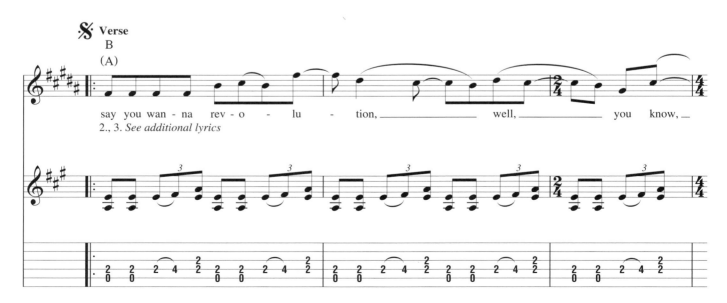

*D.S. al Coda*

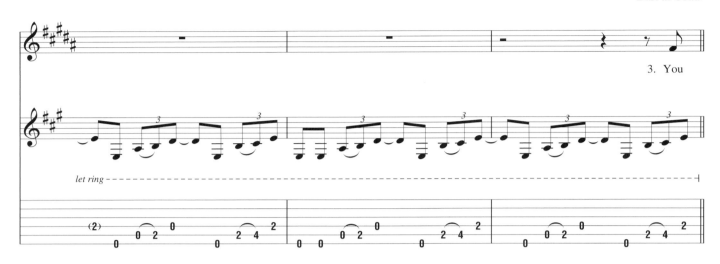

3. You

### ✛ Coda

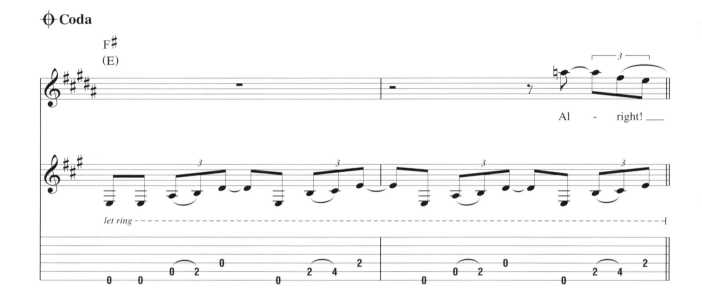

Al - right! ___

### Outro-Chorus

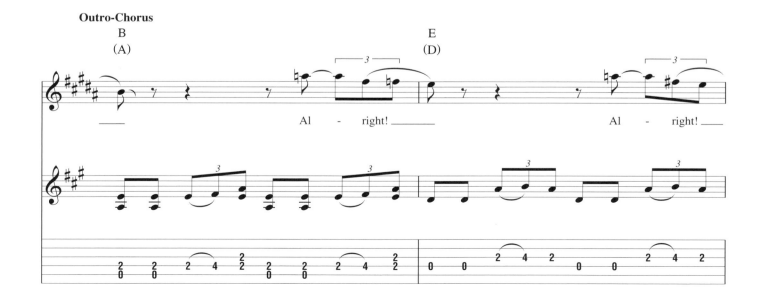

Al - right! ___ Al - right! ___

*Additional Lyrics*

2. You say you got a real solution, well, you know,
   We'd all love to see the plan.
   You ask me for a contribution, well, you know,
   We are doin' what we can.

*Pre-Chorus* 2. But if you want money for people with minds that hate,
   All I can tell you is brother, you have to wait.

3. You say you'll change the constitution, well, you know,
   We all want to change your head.
   You tell me it's the institution, well, you know,
   You better free your mind instead.

*Pre-Chorus* 3. But if you go carryin' pictures of Chairman Mao,
   Ya ain't gonna make it with anyone anyhow.

# Roxanne

Music and Lyrics by Sting

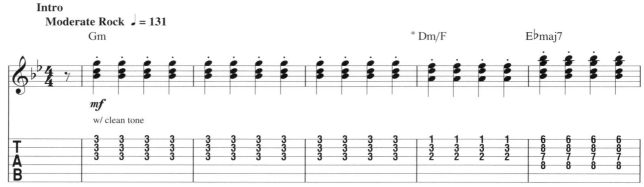

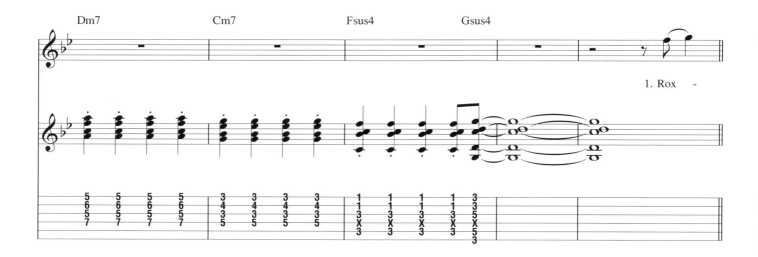

*Additional Lyrics*

2. I loved you since I knew ya,
   I wouldn't talk down to ya.
   I have to tell you just how I feel,
   I won't share you with another boy.
   I know my mind is made up,
   So put away your makeup.
   Told you once, I won't tell you again.
   It's a bad way.

# Suffragette City

Words and Music by David Bowie

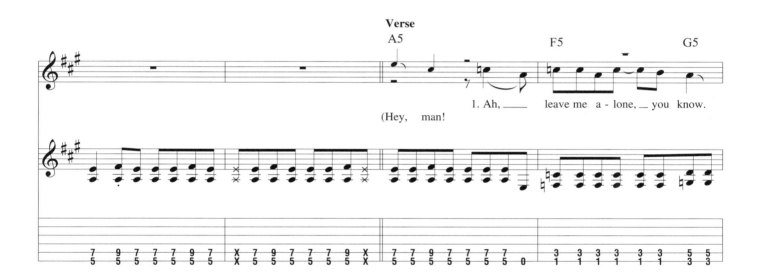

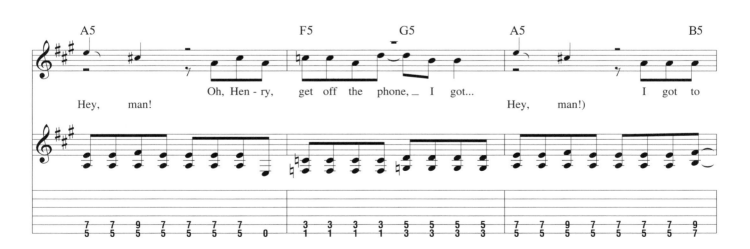

# Runnin' with the Devil

Words and Music by David Lee Roth, Edward Van Halen, Alex Van Halen and Michael Anthony

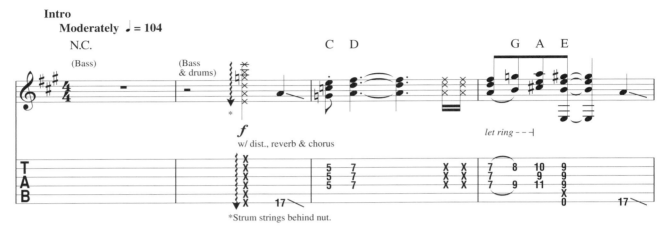

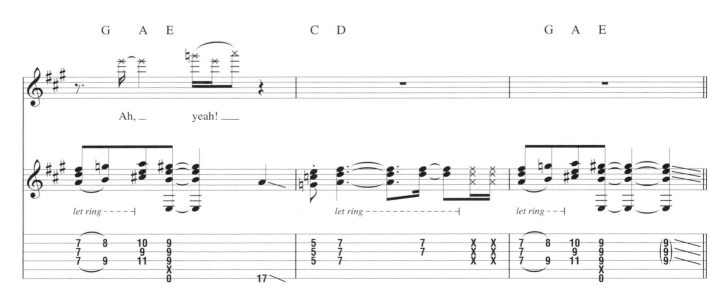

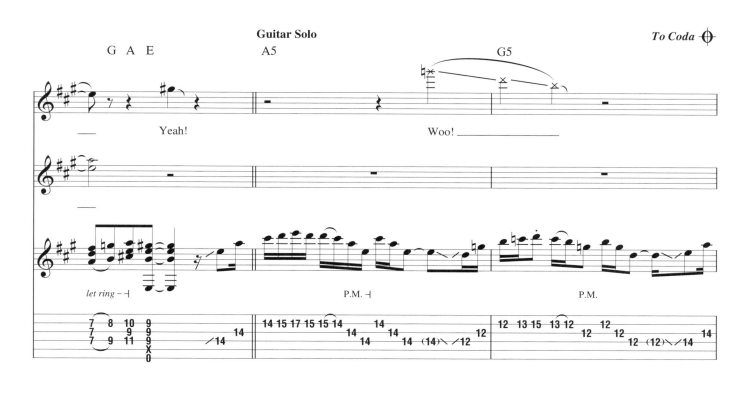

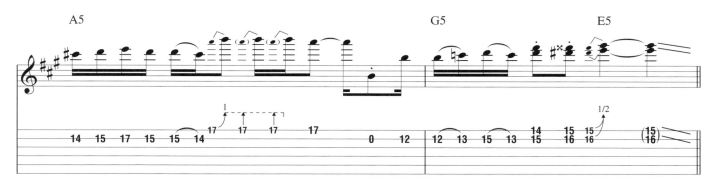

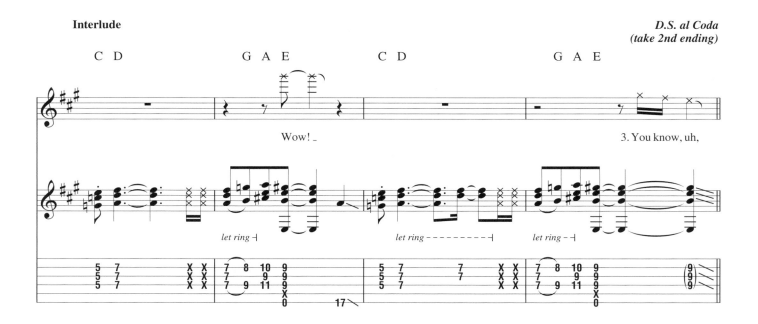

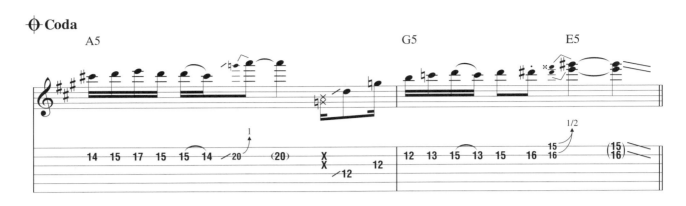

*Additional Lyrics*

2. I found the simple life ain't so simple
   When I jumped out on that road.
   I got no love, no love you'd call real.
   Ain't got nobody waitin' at home.

3. You know, uh, I found the simple life weren't so simple, no,
   When I jumped out on that road.
   Got no love, no love you'd call real.
   Got nobody waitin' at home.

# Time

Words and Music by Roger Waters, Nicholas Mason, David Gilmour and Rick Wright

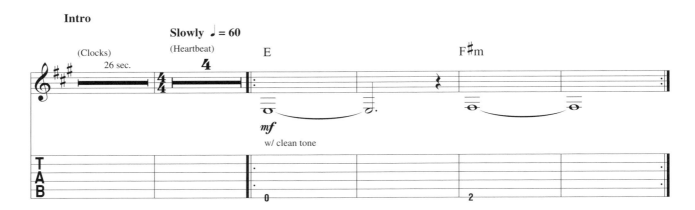

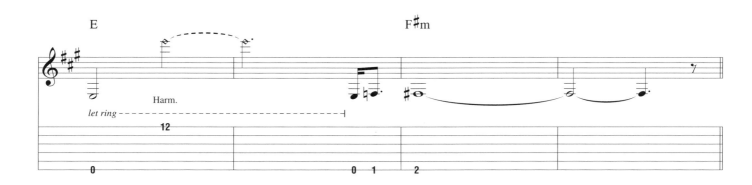

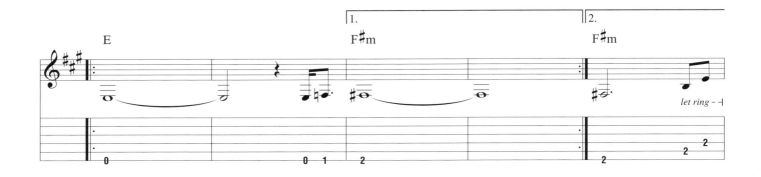

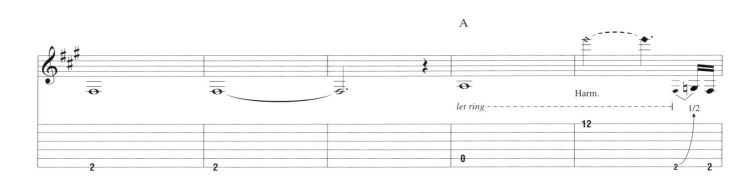

**Guitar Solo**

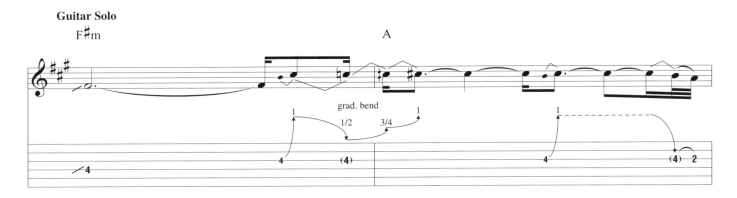

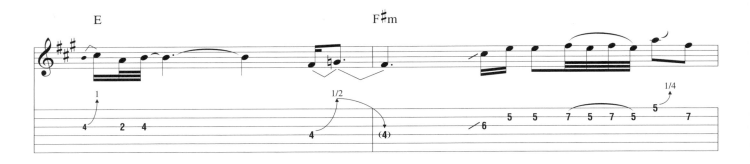

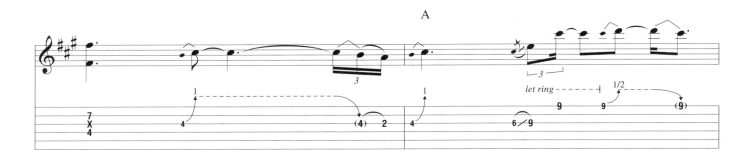

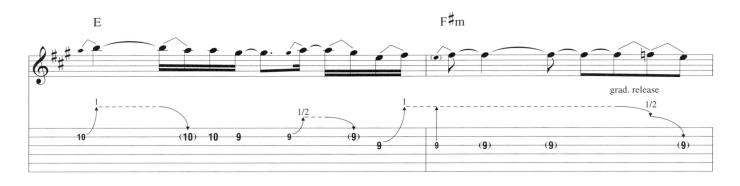

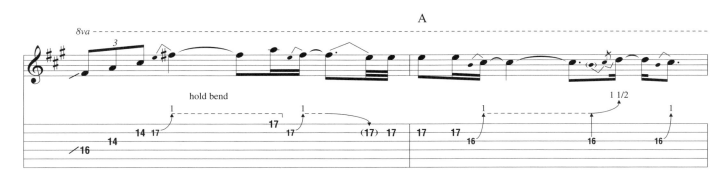

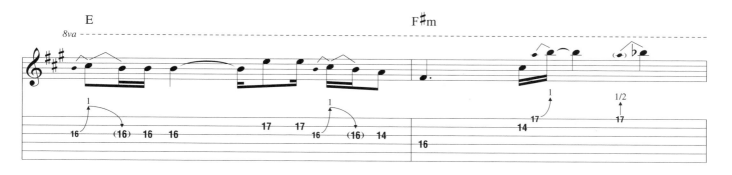

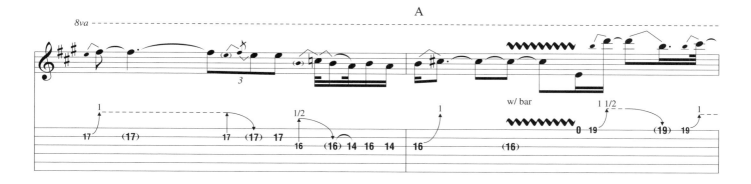

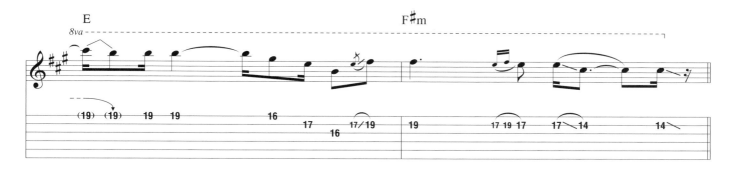

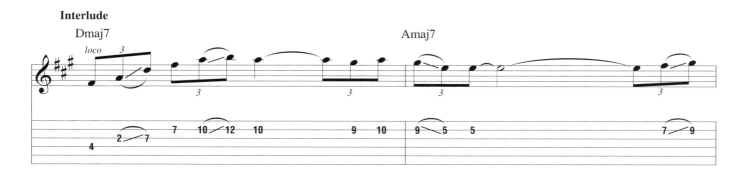

**Interlude**

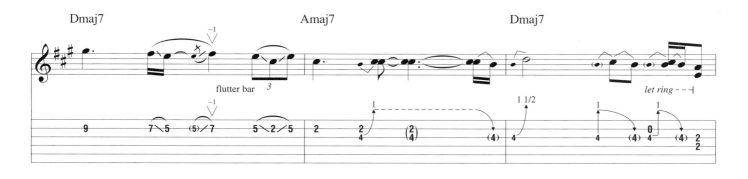

**Bridge**

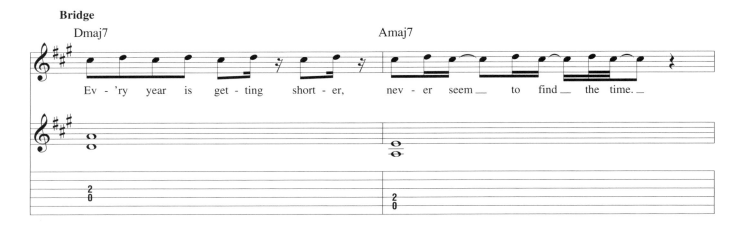

Ev - 'ry year is get - ting short - er, nev - er seem __ to find __ the time. __

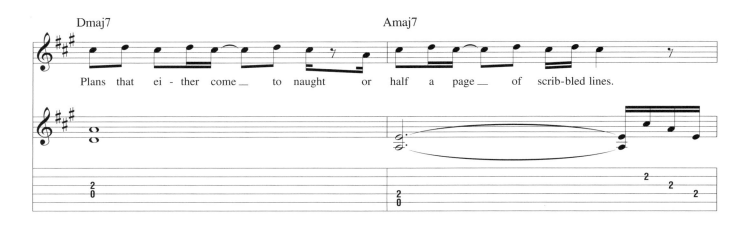

Plans that ei - ther come __ to naught or half a page __ of scrib-bled lines.

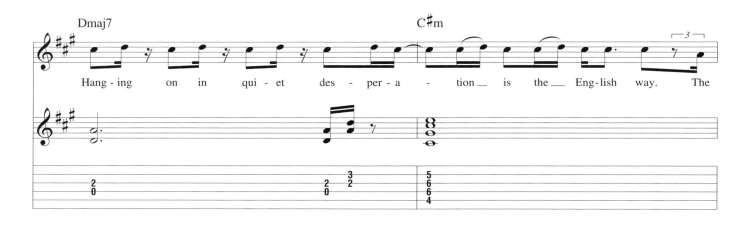

Hang - ing on in qui - et des - per - a - tion __ is the __ Eng-lish way. The

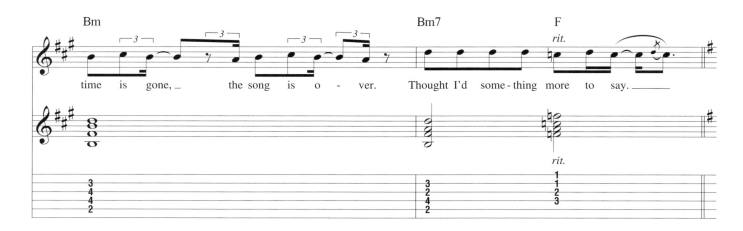

time is gone, __ the song is o - ver. Thought I'd some - thing more to say. __

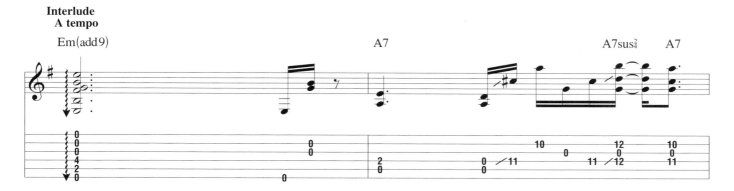

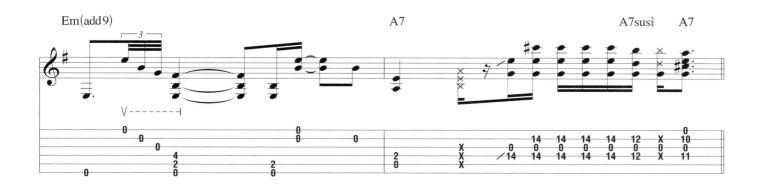

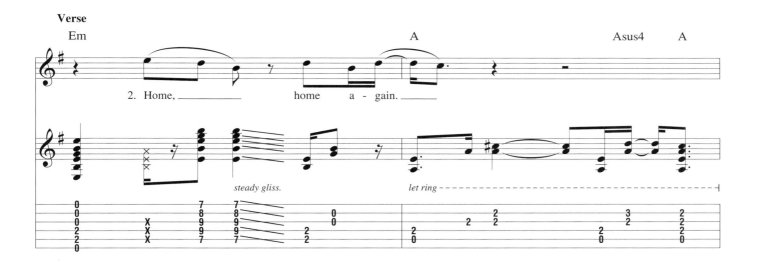

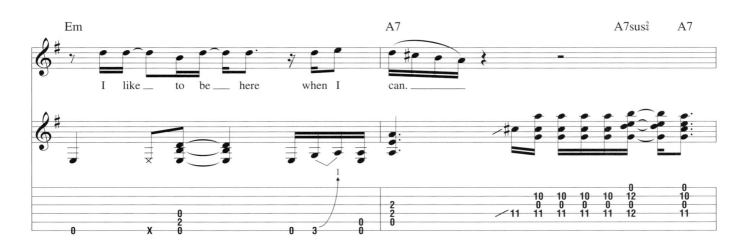

# Up Around the Bend

Words and Music by John Fogerty

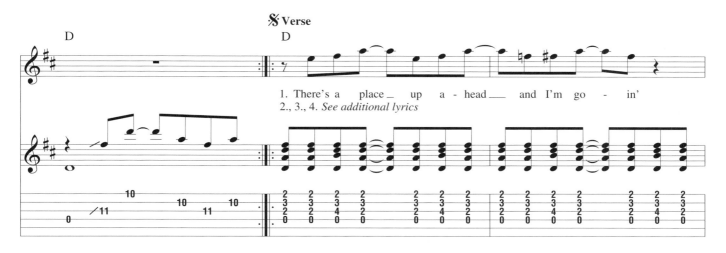

1. There's a place __ up a - head __ and I'm go - in'
2., 3., 4. *See additional lyrics*

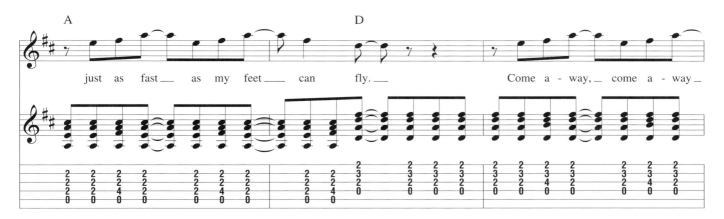

just as fast __ as my feet __ can fly. __ Come a - way, __ come a - way __

__ if you're go - in', leave the sink - in' ship __ be - hind.

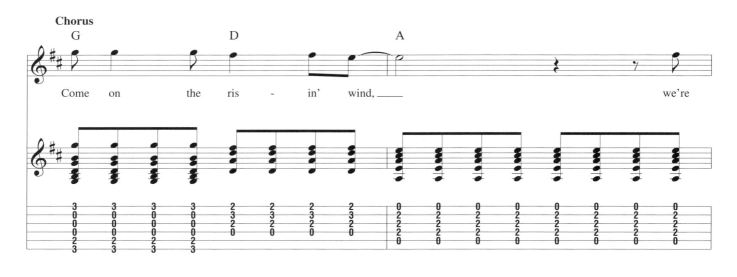

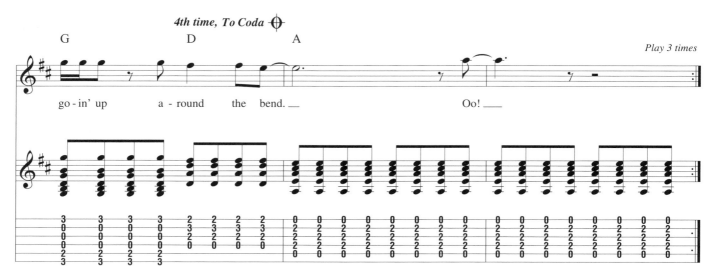

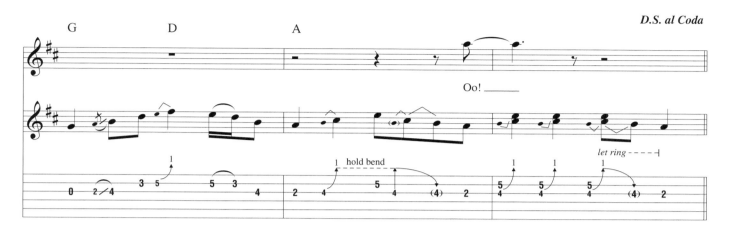

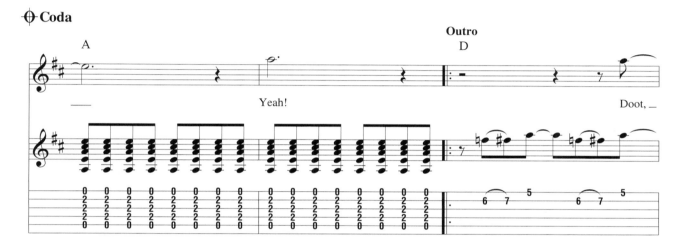

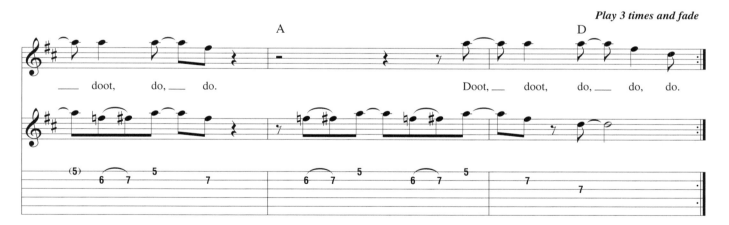

*Additional Lyrics*

2. Bring a song and a smile for the banjo.
   Better get while the gettin's good.
   Hitch a ride to the end of the highway
   Where the neons turn to wood.

3. You can ponder perpetual motion,
   Fix your mind on a crystal day.
   Always time for a good conversation,
   There's an ear for what you say.

4. Catch a ride to the end of the highway
   And we'll meet by the big red tree.
   There's a place up ahead and I'm goin';
   Come along, come along with me.

# White Room

Words and Music by Jack Bruce and Pete Brown

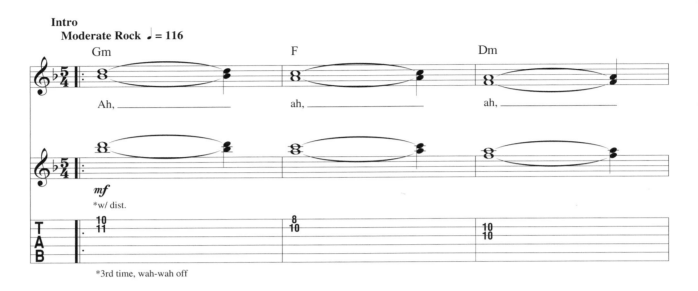

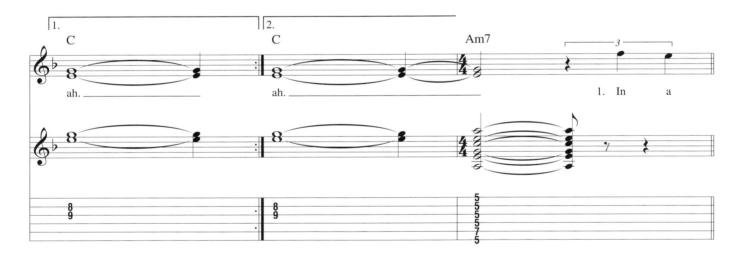

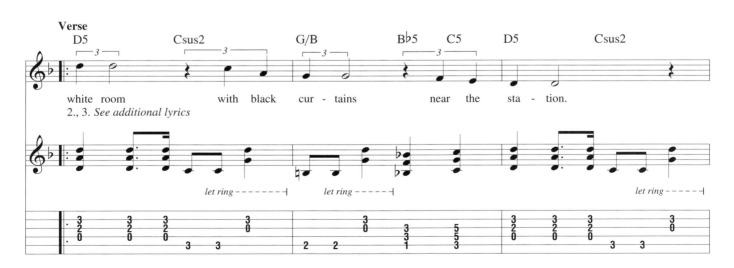

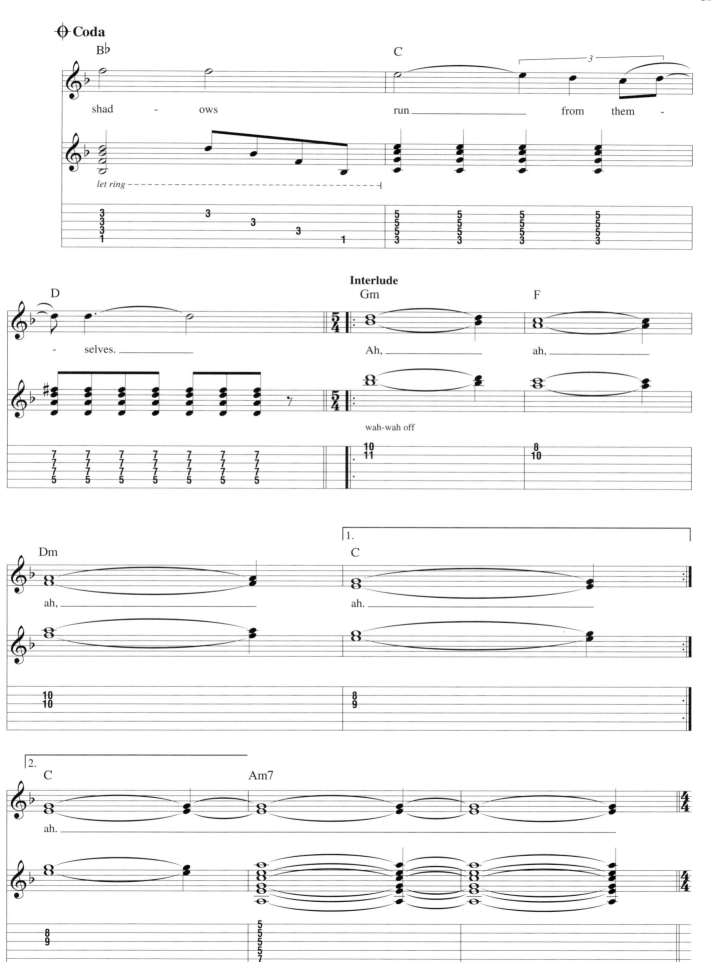

**Outro-Guitar Solo**

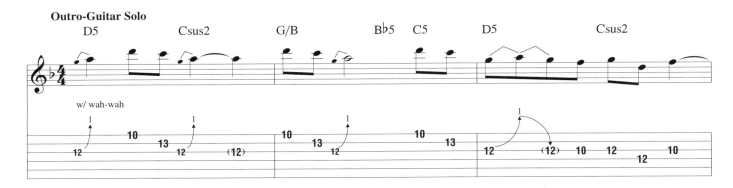

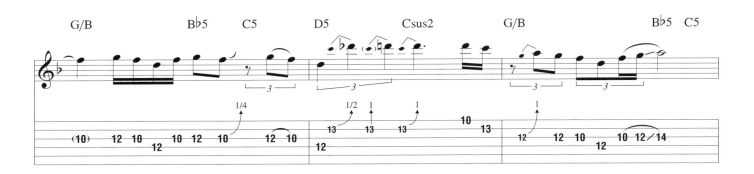

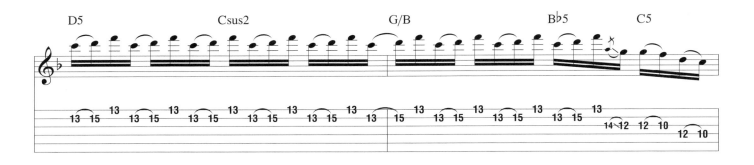

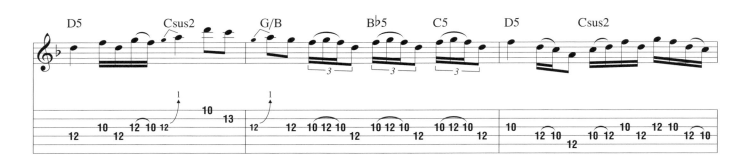

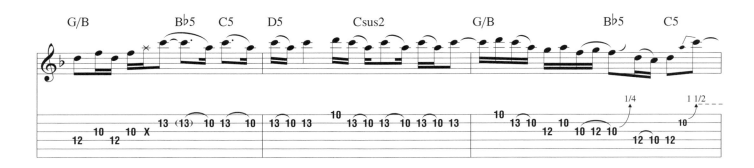

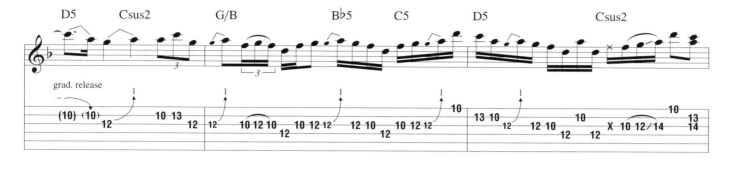

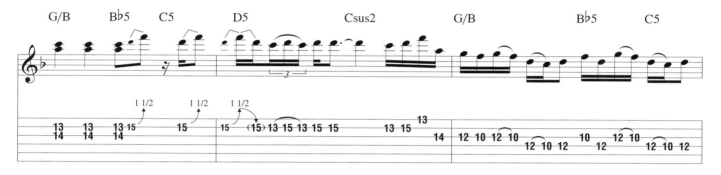

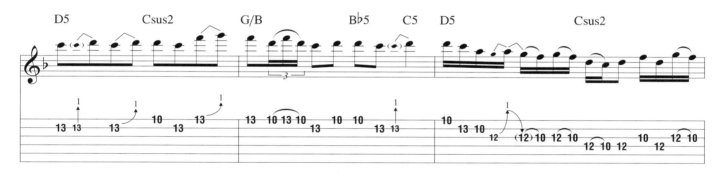

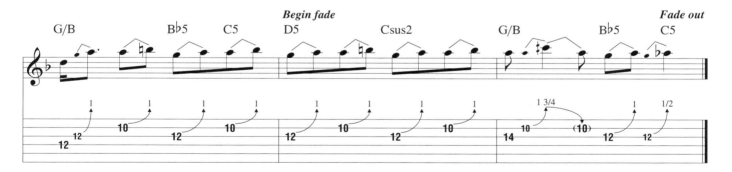

*Additional Lyrics*

2. You said no strings could secure you at the station.
Platform ticket, restless diesel, goodbye windows.
I walked into such a sad time at the station.
As I walked out felt my own need just beginning.

*Chorus* 2. I'll wait in the queue when the trains come back.
Lie with you where the shadows run from themselves.

3. At the party she was kindness in the hard crowd.
Isolation for the old queen now forgotten.
Yellow tigers crouched in jungles in her dark eyes.
She's just dressing goodbye windows, tired starling.

*Chorus* 3. I'll sleep in this place with the lonely crowd.
Lie in the dark, where the shadows run from themselves.

# War Pigs (Interpolating Luke's Wall)

Words and Music by Frank Iommi, John Osbourne, William Ward and Terence Butler

**Interlude**

N.C.(E7#9)

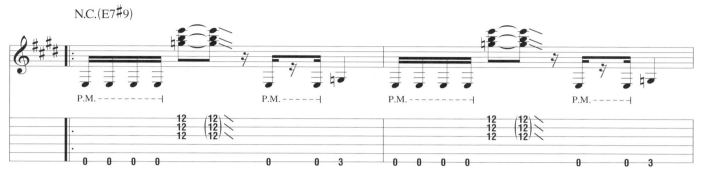

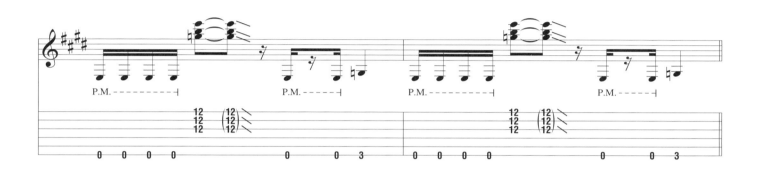

**Bridge**

N.C.(E5)

Pol - i - ti - cians hide them - selves a - way, ___
*See additional lyrics*

they on - ly start - ed the ___ war. _____

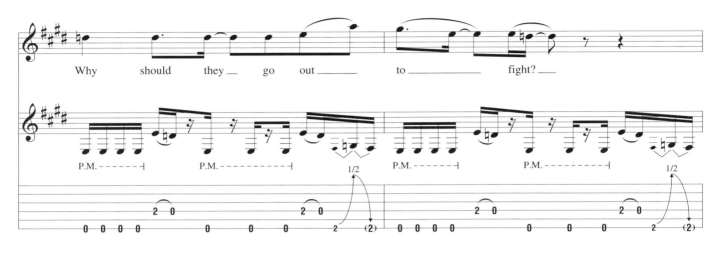

Why should they __ go out __ to _____ fight? __

They leave that __ all to the poor! __ Yeah!

**Interlude**

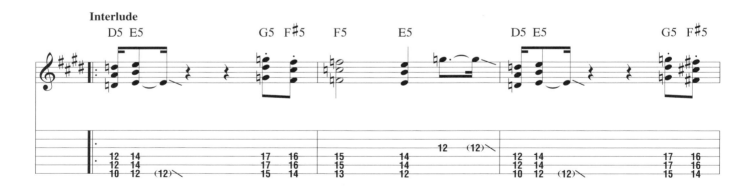

D5 E5      G5 F#5    F5     E5      D5 E5      G5 F#5

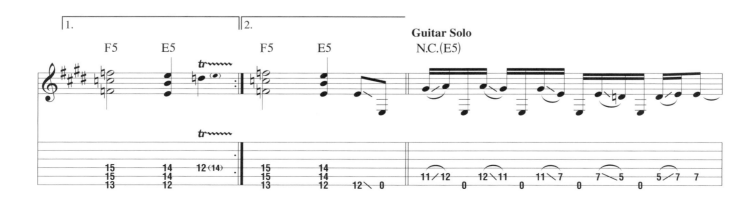

1.       2.

F5    E5      F5    E5

**Guitar Solo**

N.C.(E5)

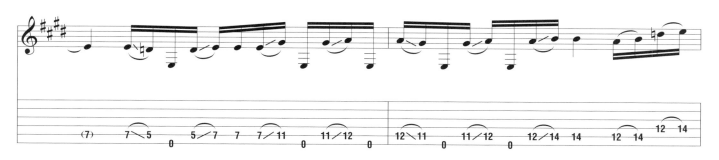

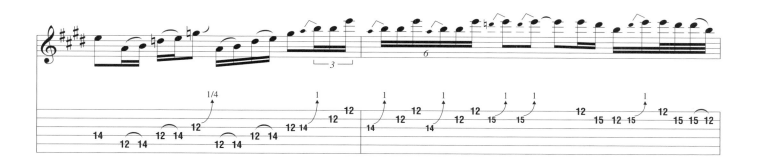

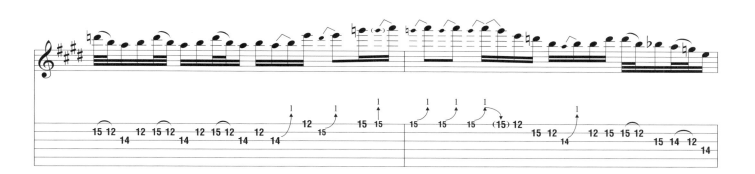

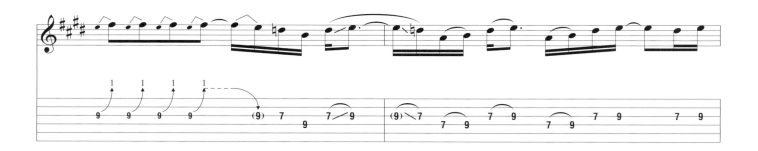

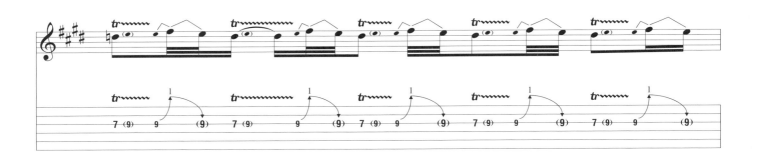

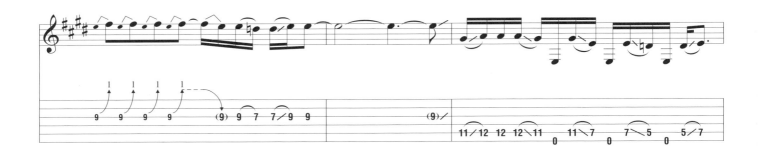

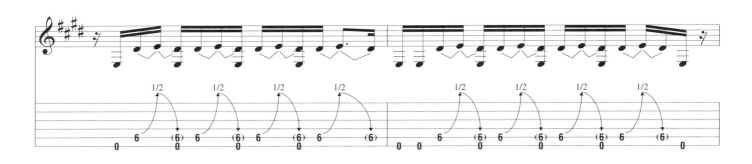

*D.S. al Coda*
*(take repeat)*

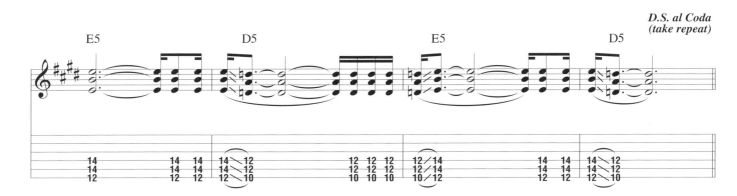

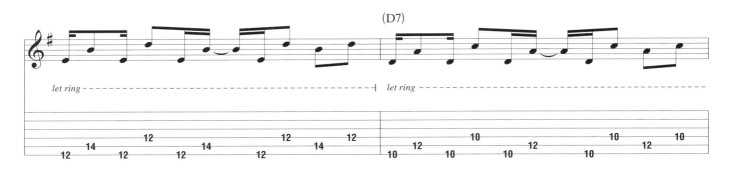

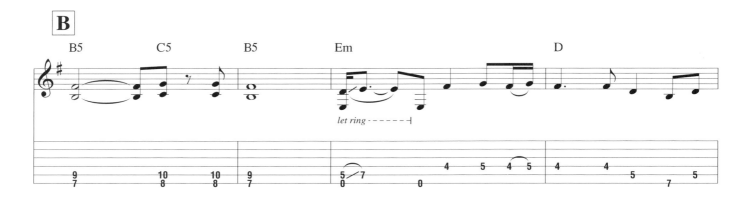

**C**

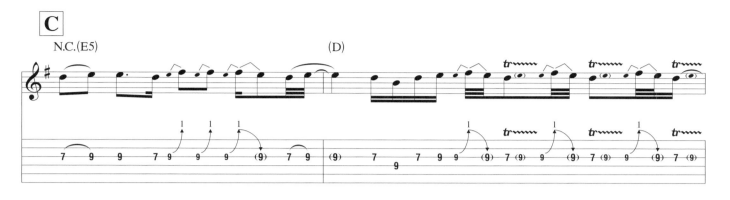

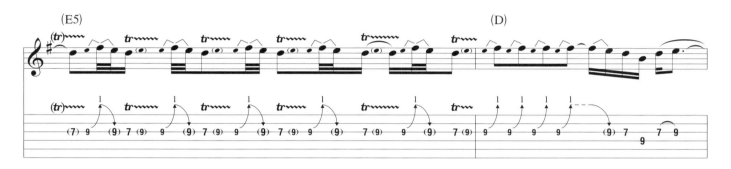

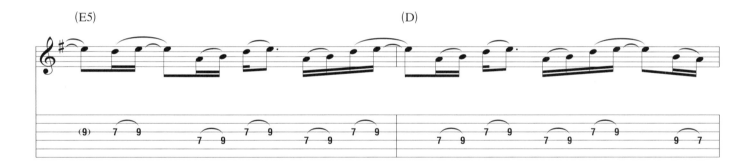

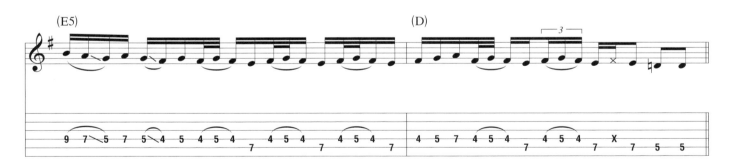

**D**

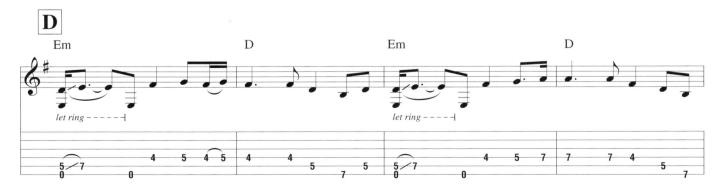

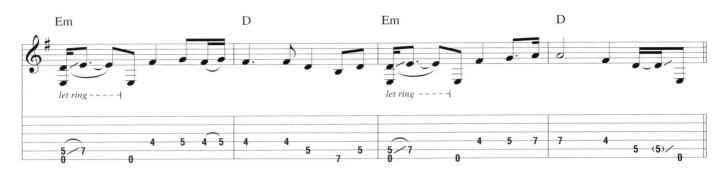

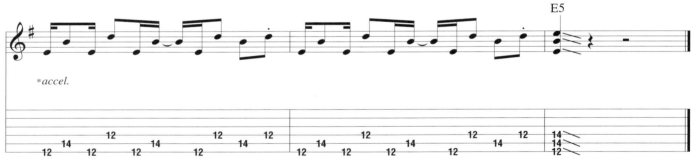

*Tape speeds up; last chord sounds 10 1/2 steps higher.

*Additional Lyrics*

2. Now in darkness, world stops turning,
   Ashes where the bodies burning.
   No more war pigs have the power.
   Hand of God has struck the hour.
   Day of judgment, God is calling,
   On their knees, the war pigs crawling.
   Begging mercies for their sins,
   Satan laughing, spreads his wings.
   Oh, Lord, yeah!

*Bridge* Time will tell on their power minds,
   Making war just for fun.
   Treating people just like pawns in chess,
   Wait till their judgment day comes. Yeah.

# Chord and Scale Charts

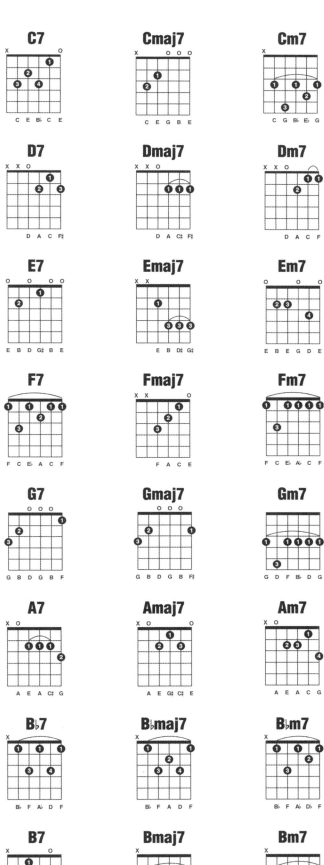
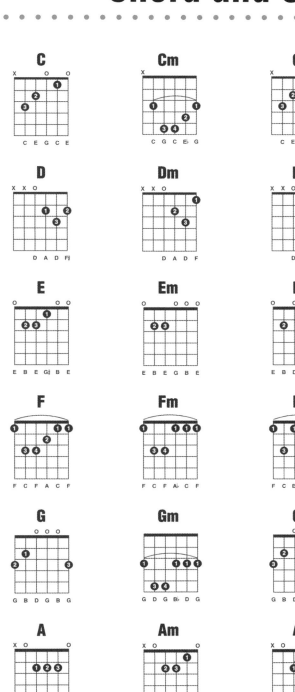
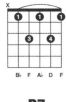
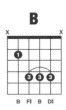
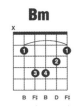

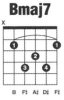

| **C** | **Cm** | **C7** | **Cmaj7** | **Cm7** |
| C E G C E | C G C E♭ G | C E B♭ C E | C E G B E | C G B♭ E♭ G |

| **D** | **Dm** | **D7** | **Dmaj7** | **Dm7** |
| D A D F♯ | D A D F | D A C F♯ | D A C♯ F♯ | D A C F |

| **E** | **Em** | **E7** | **Emaj7** | **Em7** |
| E B E G♯ B E | E B E G B E | E B D G♯ B E | E B D♯ G♯ | E B E G D E |

| **F** | **Fm** | **F7** | **Fmaj7** | **Fm7** |
| F C F A C F | F C F A♭ C F | F C E♭ A C F | A C E | F C E♭ A♭ C F |

| **G** | **Gm** | **G7** | **Gmaj7** | **Gm7** |
| G B D G B G | G D G B♭ D G | G B D G B F | G B D G B F♯ | G D F B♭ D G |

| **A** | **Am** | **A7** | **Amaj7** | **Am7** |
| A E A C♯ E | A E A C E | A E A C♯ G | A E G♯ C♯ E | A E A C G |

| **B♭** | **B♭m** | **B♭7** | **B♭maj7** | **B♭m7** |
| B♭ F B♭ D | B♭ F B♭ D♭ F | B♭ F A♭ D F | B♭ F A D F | B♭ F A♭ D♭ F |

| **B** | **Bm** | **B7** | **Bmaj7** | **Bm7** |
| B F♯ B D♯ | B F♯ B D F♯ | B D♯ A B F♯ | B F♯ A♯ D♯ F♯ | B F♯ A D F♯ |

# Power Chords

Power chords, or *5* chords, are made of two notes (the *1* and *5* intervals), sometimes stacked and repeated in different orders and octaves. "Closed" power chord positions can be played on any fret. On these diagrams the root note is circled, and notes in parentheses (●) are extra "stacked" octaves that can turn a two-note power chord into a thicker-sounding one with three or more notes. Open-position chords are rooted on the open strings.

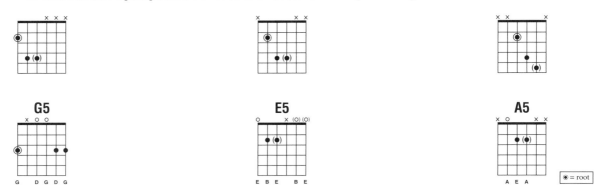

**G5**

**E5**

**A5**

G   D G D G

E B E   B E

A E A

●̲ = root

# The Minor Pentatonic Scale

The skeleton of rock riffs and solos, the minor pentatonic scale is made of five notes (penta means five), played and repeated in any order. Just like moveable power chords, you can play this scale all over the neck, depending on where the root note is. There are five *boxes* or positions of the scale — box 1 is the one you'll use the most. (A common key is A, where box 1 is rooted on fret 5.) Notice how box 2 begins where box 1 ends, and so on, so you can shift up the neck to play all five positions.

You might hear some talk of the major pentatonic scale in these pages. Think of it as the same scale, with a different root — for example, if you play box 1 as a major pentatonic scale, the top note is your root.

Want to learn to shred? Run up and down these box positions, over and over, until you can do it cleanly at blazing speed (or your neighbors start complaining).

*Box 1*

*Box 2*

*Box 3*

*Box 4*

*Box 5*

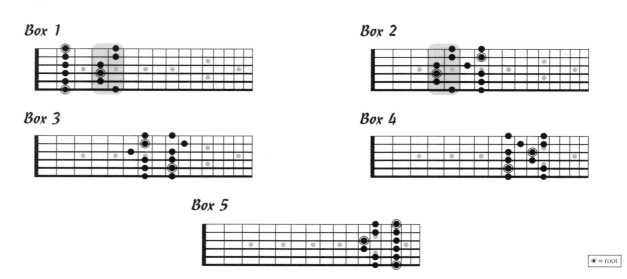

●̲ = root

# Guitar Notation Legend

Guitar Music can be notated three different ways: on a *musical staff*, in *tablature*, and in *rhythm slashes*.

**RHYTHM SLASHES** are written above the staff. Strum chords in the rhythm indicated. Use the chord diagrams found at the top of the first page of the transcription for the appropriate chord voicings. Round noteheads indicate single notes.

**THE MUSICAL STAFF** shows pitches and rhythms and is divided by bar lines into measures. Pitches are named after the first seven letters of the alphabet.

**TABLATURE** graphically represents the guitar fingerboard. Each horizontal line represents a string, and each number represents a fret.

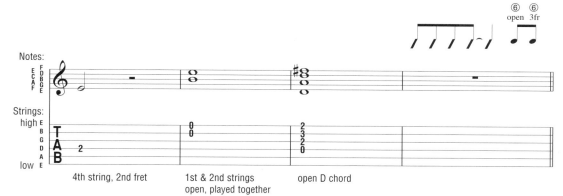

4th string, 2nd fret     1st & 2nd strings open, played together     open D chord

## Definitions for Special Guitar Notation

**HALF-STEP BEND:** Strike the note and bend up 1/2 step.

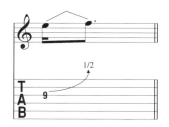

**WHOLE-STEP BEND:** Strike the note and bend up one step.

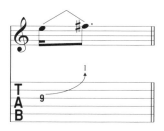

**GRACE NOTE BEND:** Strike the note and immediately bend up as indicated.

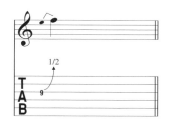

**SLIGHT (MICROTONE) BEND:** Strike the note and bend up 1/4 step.

**BEND AND RELEASE:** Strike the note and bend up as indicated, then release back to the original note. Only the first note is struck.

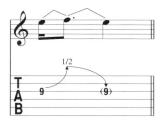

**PRE-BEND:** Bend the note as indicated, then strike it.

**PRE-BEND AND RELEASE:** Bend the note as indicated. Strike it and release the bend back to the original note.

**UNISON BEND:** Strike the two notes simultaneously and bend the lower note up to the pitch of the higher.

**VIBRATO:** The string is vibrated by rapidly bending and releasing the note with the fretting hand.

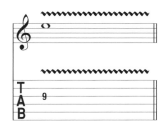

**WIDE VIBRATO:** The pitch is varied to a greater degree by vibrating with the fretting hand.

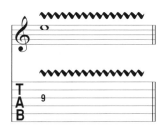

**HAMMER-ON:** Strike the first (lower) note with one finger, then sound the higher note (on the same string) with another finger by fretting it without picking.

**PULL-OFF:** Place both fingers on the notes to be sounded. Strike the first note and without picking, pull the finger off to sound the second (lower) note.

**LEGATO SLIDE:** Strike the first note and then slide the same fret-hand finger up or down to the second note. The second note is not struck.

**SHIFT SLIDE:** Same as legato slide, except the second note is struck.

**TRILL:** Very rapidly alternate between the notes indicated by continuously hammering on and pulling off.

**TAPPING:** Hammer ("tap") the fret indicated with the pick-hand index or middle finger and pull off to the note fretted by the fret hand.

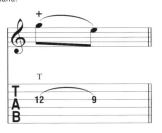

**NATURAL HARMONIC:** Strike the note while the fret-hand lightly touches the string directly over the fret indicated.

**PINCH HARMONIC:** The note is fretted normally and a harmonic is produced by adding the edge of the thumb or the tip of the index finger of the pick hand to the normal pick attack.

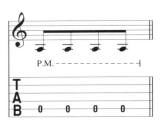

**HARP HARMONIC:** The note is fretted normally and a harmonic is produced by gently resting the pick hand's index finger directly above the indicated fret (in parentheses) while the pick hand's thumb or pick assists by plucking the appropriate string.

**PICK SCRAPE:** The edge of the pick is rubbed down (or up) the string, producing a scratchy sound.

**MUFFLED STRINGS:** A percussive sound is produced by laying the fret hand across the string(s) without depressing, and striking them with the pick hand.

**PALM MUTING:** The note is partially muted by the pick hand lightly touching the string(s) just before the bridge.

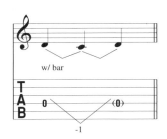

**RAKE:** Drag the pick across the strings indicated with a single motion.

**TREMOLO PICKING:** The note is picked as rapidly and continuously as possible.

**ARPEGGIATE:** Play the notes of the chord indicated by quickly rolling them from bottom to top.

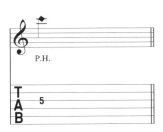

**VIBRATO BAR DIVE AND RETURN:** The pitch of the note or chord is dropped a specified number of steps (in rhythm), then returned to the original pitch.

**VIBRATO BAR SCOOP:** Depress the bar just before striking the note, then quickly release the bar.

**VIBRATO BAR DIP:** Strike the note and then immediately drop a specified number of steps, then release back to the original pitch.

# Additional Musical Definitions

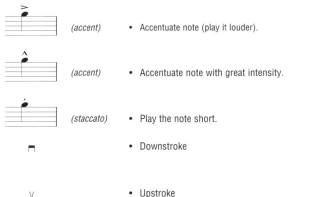

| | | |
|---|---|---|
| (accent) | • | Accentuate note (play it louder). |
| (accent) | • | Accentuate note with great intensity. |
| (staccato) | • | Play the note short. |
| | • | Downstroke |
| V | • | Upstroke |
| *D.S. al Coda* | • | Go back to the sign (%), then play until the measure marked "*To Coda*," then skip to the section labelled "**Coda**." |
| *D.C. al Fine* | • | Go back to the beginning of the song and play until the measure marked "*Fine*" (end). |

| | | |
|---|---|---|
| **Rhy. Fig.** | • | Label used to recall a recurring accompaniment pattern (usually chordal). |
| **Riff** | • | Label used to recall composed, melodic lines (usually single notes) which recur. |
| **Fill** | • | Label used to identify a brief melodic figure which is to be inserted into the arrangement. |
| **Rhy. Fill** | • | A chordal version of a Fill. |
| tacet | • | Instrument is silent (drops out). |
| | • | Repeat measures between signs. |
| | • | When a repeated section has different endings, play the first ending only the first time and the second ending only the second time. |

**NOTE:** Tablature numbers in parentheses mean:
1. The note is being sustained over a system (note in standard notation is tied), or
2. The note is sustained, but a new articulation (such as a hammer-on, pull-off, slide or vibrato) begins, or
3. The note is a barely audible "ghost" note (note in standard notation is also in parentheses).

# HAL•LEONARD GUITAR PLAY-ALONG

This series will help you play your favorite songs quickly and easily. Just follow the tab and listen to the CD to hear how the guitar should sound, and then play along using the separate backing tracks. Mac or PC users can also slow down the tempo without changing pitch by using the CD in their computer. The melody and lyrics are included in the book so that you can sing or simply follow along.

| | | | |
|---|---|---|---|
| **. ROCK**<br>0699570 ..........$16.99 | **15. R&B**<br>00699583..........$14.95 | **29. BOB SEGER**<br>00699647..........$14.95 | **43. LYNYRD SKYNYRD**<br>00699681..........$17.95 |
| **. ACOUSTIC**<br>0699569..........$16.95 | **16. JAZZ**<br>00699584..........$15.95 | **30. KISS**<br>00699644..........$14.95 | **44. JAZZ**<br>00699689..........$14.95 |
| **. HARD ROCK**<br>0699573..........$16.95 | **17. COUNTRY**<br>00699588..........$15.95 | **31. CHRISTMAS HITS**<br>00699652..........$14.95 | **45. TV THEMES**<br>00699718..........$14.95 |
| **. POP/ROCK**<br>0699571..........$16.99 | **18. ACOUSTIC ROCK**<br>00699577..........$15.95 | **32. THE OFFSPRING**<br>00699653..........$14.95 | **46. MAINSTREAM ROCK**<br>00699722..........$16.95 |
| **. MODERN ROCK**<br>0699574..........$16.99 | **19. SOUL**<br>00699578..........$14.95 | **33. ACOUSTIC CLASSICS**<br>00699656..........$16.95 | **47. HENDRIX SMASH HITS**<br>00699723..........$19.95 |
| **. '90s ROCK**<br>0699572..........$16.99 | **20. ROCKABILLY**<br>00699580..........$14.95 | **34. CLASSIC ROCK**<br>00699658..........$16.95 | **48. AEROSMITH CLASSICS**<br>00699724..........$16.99 |
| **. BLUES**<br>0699575..........$16.95 | **21. YULETIDE**<br>00699602..........$14.95 | **35. HAIR METAL**<br>00699660..........$16.95 | **49. STEVIE RAY VAUGHAN**<br>00699725..........$16.95 |
| **. ROCK**<br>0699585..........$12.95 | **22. CHRISTMAS**<br>00699600..........$15.95 | **36. SOUTHERN ROCK**<br>00699661..........$16.95 | **50. NÜ METAL**<br>00699726..........$14.95 |
| **. PUNK ROCK**<br>0699576..........$14.95 | **23. SURF**<br>00699635..........$14.95 | **37. ACOUSTIC METAL**<br>00699662..........$16.95 | **51. ALTERNATIVE '90s**<br>00699727..........$12.95 |
| **. ACOUSTIC**<br>99586..........$16.95 | **24. ERIC CLAPTON**<br>00699649..........$16.95 | **38. BLUES**<br>00699663..........$16.95 | **52. FUNK**<br>00699728..........$14.95 |
| **EARLY ROCK**<br>579..........$14.95 | **25. LENNON & McCARTNEY**<br>00699642 ..........$14.95 | **39. '80s METAL**<br>00699664..........$16.99 | **53. DISCO**<br>00699729..........$14.99 |
| **OP/ROCK**<br>87..........$14.95 | **26. ELVIS PRESLEY**<br>00699643..........$14.95 | **40. INCUBUS**<br>00699668..........$17.95 | **54. HEAVY METAL**<br>00699730..........$14.95 |
| **K ROCK**<br>..........$14.95 | **27. DAVID LEE ROTH**<br>00699645..........$16.95 | **41. ERIC CLAPTON**<br>00699669..........$16.95 | **55. POP METAL**<br>00699731..........$14.95 |
| **ROCK**<br>..........$16.95 | **28. GREG KOCH**<br>00699646..........$14.95 | **42. CHART HITS**<br>00699670..........$16.95 | **56. FOO FIGHTERS**<br>00699749..........$14.95 |

*Prices, contents, and availability
subject to change without notice.*

FOR MORE INFORMATION,
SEE YOUR LOCAL MUSIC DEALER,
OR WRITE TO:

HAL•LEONARD
CORPORATION
7777 W. BLUEMOUND RD. P.O.
MILWAUKEE, WISCONSIN

For complete so
visit Hal Leonar
www.halleo

# GUITAR PLAY-ALONG

This series will help you play your favorite songs quickly and easily. Just follow the tab and listen to the CD to hear how the guitar should sound, and then play along using the separate backing tracks. Mac or PC users can also slow down the tempo without changing pitch by using the CD in their computer. The melody and lyrics are included in the book so that you can sing or simply follow along.

**INCLUDES TAB**

| | | | |
|---|---|---|---|
| **57. SYSTEM OF A DOWN**<br>00699751.............................$14.95 | **71. CHRISTIAN ROCK**<br>00699824.............................$14.95 | **87. ACOUSTIC WOMEN**<br>00700763 ..........................$14.99 | **111. JOHN MELLENCAMP**<br>00701056.............................$14.99 |
| **58. BLINK-182**<br>00699772.............................$14.95 | **72. ACOUSTIC '90s**<br>00699827.............................$14.95 | **88. GRUNGE**<br>00700467 ..........................$16.99 | **113. JIM CROCE**<br>00701058.............................$14.99 |
| **59. GODSMACK**<br>00699773.............................$14.95 | **73. BLUESY ROCK**<br>00699829 .........................$16.99 | **91. BLUES INSTRUMENTALS**<br>00700505 ..........................$14.99 | **114. BON JOVI**<br>00701060 .........................$14.99 |
| **60. 3 DOORS DOWN**<br>00699774.............................$14.95 | **74. PAUL BALOCHE**<br>00699831.............................$14.95 | **92. EARLY ROCK INSTRUMENTALS**<br>00700506 ..........................$12.99 | **115. JOHNNY CASH**<br>00701070 .........................$14.99 |
| **61. SLIPKNOT**<br>00699775.............................$14.95 | **75. TOM PETTY**<br>00699882.............................$16.99 | **93. ROCK INSTRUMENTALS**<br>00700507 ..........................$14.99 | **116. THE VENTURES**<br>00701124 .........................$14.99 |
| **62. CHRISTMAS CAROLS**<br>00699798.............................$12.95 | **76. COUNTRY HITS**<br>00699884.............................$14.95 | **96. THIRD DAY**<br>00700560 ..........................$14.95 | **119. AC/DC CLASSICS**<br>00701356 .........................$14.95 |
| **63. CREEDENCE CLEARWATER REVIVAL**<br>00699802.............................$16.99 | **78. NIRVANA**<br>00700132.............................$14.95 | **97. ROCK BAND**<br>00700703.............................$14.99 | |
| **64. OZZY OSBOURNE**<br>00699803.............................$16.99 | **88. ACOUSTIC ANTHOLOGY**<br>00700175.............................$19.95 | **98. ROCK BAND**<br>00700704.............................$14.95 | *Prices, contents, and availability<br>subject to change without notice.* |
| **65. THE DOORS**<br>00699806.............................$16.99 | **81. ROCK ANTHOLOGY**<br>00700176.............................$22.99 | **99. ZZ TOP**<br>00700762 ..........................$14.99 | FOR MORE INFORMATION,<br>SEE YOUR LOCAL MUSIC DEALER,<br>OR WRITE TO: |
| **66. THE ROLLING STONES**<br>00699807.............................$16.95 | **82. EASY ROCK SONGS**<br>00700177.............................$12.99 | **100. B.B. KING**<br>00700466 ..........................$14.99 | |
| **67. BLACK SABBATH**<br>00699808.............................$16.99 | **83. THREE CHORD SONGS**<br>00700178.............................$14.99 | **103. SWITCHFOOT**<br>00700773 ..........................$16.99 |  |
| **68. PINK FLOYD –**<br>**DARK SIDE OF THE MOON**<br>00699809.............................$16.99 | **84. STEELY DAN**<br>00700200 .........................$16.99 | **106. WEEZER**<br>00700958 ..........................$14.99 | HAL•LEONARD®<br>CORPORATION |
| **69. ACOUSTIC FAVORITES**<br>00699810.............................$14.95 | **85. THE POLICE**<br>00700269 .........................$16.99 | **108. THE WHO**<br>00701053 ..........................$14.99 | 7777 W. BLUEMOUND RD. P.O. BOX 13819<br>MILWAUKEE, WISCONSIN 53213 |
| **70. OZZY OSBOURNE**<br>00699805 ...........................$16.99 | **86. BOSTON**<br>00700465 .........................$16.99 | **109. STEVE MILLER**<br>00701054 ..........................$14.99 | **For complete songlists,<br>visit Hal Leonard online at<br>www.halleonard.com** |

0710